5 to 8

Environmental Issues

FACING THE CHALLENGES

Published by World Teachers Press®

www.worldteacherspress.com

Order Number: 2-5289
ISBN-13: 978-1-58324-271-1

A B C D E F 11 10 09 08 07

395 Main Street
Rowley, MA 01969
www.didax.com

Foreword

Environmental Issues is one of a series of four books designed specifically for middle school students.

Environmental Issues provides a comprehensive overview of contemporary problems relating to the state of the environment: pollution; deforestation; biodiversity; conservation; endangered species; energy sources; global warming; ozone depletion; soil degradation; genetically modified foods; urbanization; natural disasters; recycling, reducing and reusing; pesticides; hazardous waste and water resources.

Titles in this series:
- *Natural Disasters*
- *Rainforests*
- *Antarctica*
- *Environmental Issues*

The book challenges students to consider the results of human activities and gives some information regarding the causes, effects and possible solutions to the problems.

The widely-varied activities in this book cross all major learning areas.

Contents

The 16 environmental issues covered in this book are presented in a similar format:

Each environmental issue is divided into a unit of four pages:

- a teacher page
- a student information page
- a student comprehension page
- a cross-curricular activity.

An **overview** for teachers has been included on pages 6–9 with suggestions for activities to further develop the theme with the whole class or as extension work for more able students.

Teacher Page

The teacher page has the following information:

Indicators state literacy outcomes for reading and comprehending the informational text and outcomes relating to the cross-curricular student page.

Page numbers for **Quiz Questions** relating to the section are given in the Worksheet Information section.

Answers are given for all questions, where applicable. Open-ended tasks require the teacher to check the answers.

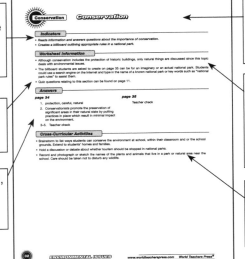

The **Title of the Text** indicates the environmental issue or one example of that particular environmental issue.

Worksheet Information details any background information required by the teacher about the environmental issue, or presents specific details regarding the use of the worksheets.

Cross-Curricular Activities suggest further means to develop the topic in the same, or another, learning area.

In some cases, Web sites or specific URLs may be recommended. While these are checked and rechecked at the time of publication, the publisher has no control over any subsequent changes which may be made to Web pages. It is *strongly* recommended that the class teacher checks *all* URLs before allowing students to access them.

Quiz Questions

Quiz questions with answers are given for each section on pages 10 to 19.

The quiz questions are presented in a "half-page" card format for ease of photocopying and may be:

- given orally, with students answering on a separate sheet of paper,
- photocopied and given individually as a written test,
- combined with the other apropriate pages for the unit(s) as a final assessment of the topic, or
- photocopied and used by pairs or groups of students as "quick quiz" activities.

The student pages follow the format below.

- The first student page is an informational text, providing general information about each environmental issue, its causes and consequences, and artwork where appropriate.

- The second student page is a comprehension page to gauge student understanding of the text. A variety of activities is provided, including answering literal, inferential and applied questions, compiling information for a retrieval chart, completing diagrams or maps, and cloze activities.

- The final student page is a cross-curricular activity. Sometimes, these activities may fall within the same learning area, such as English.

Student Pages

1.

Informational Text about the particular issue is provided.

The Title of the environmental issue is given.

Diagrams that assist in explaining the particular issue are included, if appropriate.

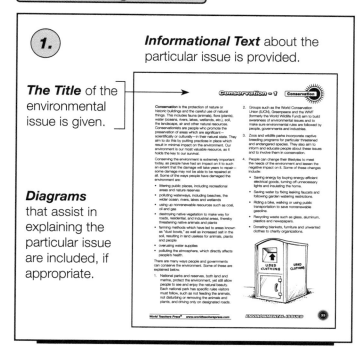

2.

The Title of the issue

Comprehension Activities are provided to gauge student understanding.

Fact File: An interesting fact is included on student pages 2 and 3 to extend knowledge.

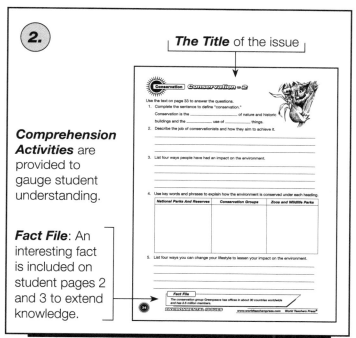

3.

The Title reflects the type of activity to be completed.

Answers are provided for this page if needed.

Fact File: An interesting fact is included on student pages 2 and 3 to extend knowledge.

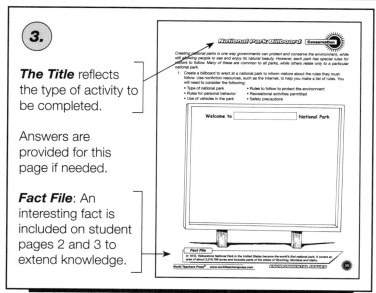

The cross-curricular activities suggested below may aid in developing the theme.

English

- "Interview" an animal from a particular endangered species to discover how it is struggling to survive.

- Read information and write a report about a specific environmental problem, offering some practical suggestions for ways to alleviate the problem.

- Collect and collate newspaper articles about a given environmental issue and update information as it is supplied; for example, a tanker oil spill, water resource situations, building in eco-sensitive areas.

- Use the letters in large words such as "environment," "deforestation," "conservation" and "urbanization" to write a list of smaller words.

- Construct a word puzzle using words associated with pollution.

- Debate the topic: "Fertilizers should be banned."

- Write a poem about the environmental issue of greatest personal concern to individual students.

- Write a newspaper report about a current environmental issue of concern to the local community.

- Write an "eyewitness" account from a native animal's point of view of it watching its habitat being destroyed to make way for housing.

- Write a playscript about an environmental issue; include some ways to improve the problem.

- Write and illustrate a book about an environmental issue suitable for a lower elementary student to read; e.g., the importance of recycling or why an animal is endangered.

Math

- Record and graph daily UV levels over a given time and, if possible, compare to those of ten or 20 years ago.

- Collect data and record information about the various ways classmates conserve water and energy in their home.

- Collect data and make color-coded maps to represent changes to a particular environment such as the Amazon Rainforest.

- Classify environmental problems as "solvable" or "able to be improved" and list achievable suggestions for each.

- Research to find and graph the cost per gallon of different bottled waters.

- Calculate the cost per gallon of tap water.

- Over a week, tally the number of glasses or cups of each different type of beverage consumed daily by the class.

- Research the cost of electricity and gas in your community and compare it with another. Explain possible differences in cost.

- Record the variations in fuel prices at a number of sources in the community over one month to determine which is cheapest.

- Calculate the cost per 100 miles for fuel for the family car. Compare your results. Which car is the most economical and which is the most expensive?

- Students compare their family's gas, electricity and water bills at different times of the year. Why are they higher at certain times of the year? What could they do to lower the bill?

- Collect data for a pie graph to show types of energy used by students' families for heating, cooling and cooking.

- Tally the type of litter found at various places in the school and local community.

- Find out the numbers remaining of selected endangered species.

The cross-curricular activities suggested below may aid in developing the theme.

Social Studies

- Research the varieties of plants and animals within a specific environment to reinforce the concept of biodiversity.

- Investigate environmental issues relating to specific periods in history, such as during the exploration of the Amazon.

- Locate on a map and plot a path to reach a local recycling or landfill facility.

- Create a time line which shows the increase in pollution levels over the last 50 years.

- Research irrigation and write a report on possible water conservation measures that could be introduced.

- Investigate your local water supply to determine where it comes from and what treatment it has before you drink it.

- Research a fertilizer used in your garden: why it is used, how often, the cost, its effectiveness and how toxic it is.

- Research how electricity is produced in your community.

- Describe ways different natural disasters affect the environment; e.g., floods cause soil erosion.

- Investigate how various organizations help with environmental issues; e.g., Greenpeace and WWF.

- Locate and label on a map 20 of the world's largest cities. Identify environmental issues that result from urbanization.

- Observe how the school reduces, reuses and recycles materials and suggest any improvements that could be made.

Science

- Conduct experiments to investigate the amount of pollution in the air and water in the school and local environment.

- Devise and conduct simple experiments to investigate alternate sources of energy such as heat from decaying vegetable matter, wind power, etc.

- Draw charts, diagrams and tables which show changes to a natural system due to an introduced environmental issue.

- Collect data and draw conclusions about changes to the atmosphere caused by a specific human activity.

- Research desalination and write a report detailing what it is, how it works and any environmental concerns associated with it.

- Explain "acid rain" and how it affects the paint on cars in large cities.

- Asbestos is a dangerous substance. Research the effects it has on the human body.

- Explain the term "radioactive."

- Investigate wind erosion by blowing a hair dryer over a tray of dirt and sand and a tray of rocks, sand, dirt and twigs. Compare results. Change the angles of the trays; also use wet and dry soil.

- Record animal and plant life in an area near the school, then check again in six months. Compare results and give reasons for any differences.

- Research the negative effects plastic bags can have on the environment; e.g., turtles think they are jellyfish and swallow them — they can choke on them or they block their stomach so they can't eat.

The cross-curricular activities suggested below may aid in developing the theme.

The Arts (Music, Drama, Visual Arts)

- Design posters highlighting an environmental issue and offering practical suggestions for combating the problem.

- In groups, dramatize the process of trees being cut down, the effects on animals and other vegetation and possible solutions.

- Create percussion pieces to accompany a poem or song about an environmental issue.

- Design and make two dioramas — one showing before and the other after an environmental change.

- Create a collage to demonstrate the dangers associated with pesticides.

- Mime an environmental issue for others to identify.

- Dramatize a discussion about conservation of Earth's resources between a driver of a large car and the driver of a very small, economical car.

- Learn a song about an environmental issue; e.g., *Blue Sky Mine* by Midnight Oil.

- Make up a list of energy-saving ideas and mime the actions for other students to guess; e.g., checking the seal on the fridge to make sure that it is closing properly.

- Role-play a protest march for an environmental problem, such as a local lake becoming polluted with plastic bags and cans or a bypass road being built through a wildlife reserve.

- Draw pictures of what students think a built-up area looked like in its natural state and comment on any environmental issues.

- Create an environmental soundscape about an issue; e.g., a polluted environment, farmland affected by drought.

- Use various art and craft techniques to create scenes depicting natural disasters.

PE/Health and Values

- Following a visit to a supermarket, investigate and record information about genetically-modified foods.

- Interview class members regarding health issues such as allergies caused by pollution or hazardous materials.

- Conduct research to determine how health issues have developed as a direct result of changes to the environment.

- Discuss motivations or values relating to commercialism vs. conserving diminishing resources, satisfying the demand for wood products vs. conserving the habitat of indigenous people, etc.

- Research and list health problems related to air and water pollution.

- Investigate medical problems attributed to a particular hazardous waste.

- Research food additives which have been linked to cancer.

- Investigate the advantages and disadvantages of adding chlorine to drinking water.

- Fluoride is added to some water supplies. Investigate why, how effective it is, and any health concerns there are about it.

- Organize with the principal for the school to practice fire and earthquake drills.

- Invite a guest speaker to talk about the importance of conserving water, conserving nonrenewable resources, or developing renewable resources.

- Discuss the dangers of swimming in water infected with algal bloom or high concentrations of particular chemicals.

The cross-curricular activities suggested below may aid in developing the theme.

Technology and Enterprise

- Design simple devices for measuring air and water pollution.

- Investigate the effects advances in technology and industry may have on the environment.

- Investigate the materials used as insulation or packaging and offer more environmentally-friendly choices.

- Investigate the Web sites of organizations that aim to develop awareness of endangered species or specific environmental issues.

- Research specifications for a rain gauge and construct one suitable for use at school.

- Design a fly trap that could be used instead of pesticide to reduce fly numbers.

- Devise and conduct an experiment to demonstrate evaporation.

- Investigate a "natural" pesticide that is harmless to people, plants and domestic pets. Write instructions for making this pesticide. Design appropriate packaging and labelling.

- Design a model of a compost bin.

- Investigate how technology enables scientists to predict or monitor potential disasters such as cyclones, earthquakes and volcanoes.

- Design a protective suit to wear when handling hazardous waste. Draw and label it.

- Design and construct a model of an environmentally-friendly housing tract. Consider water resources, native vegetation, renewable energy sources, etc.

1. Check the true statements.

    (a) Only humans can care for and destroy the Earth's natural resources. ☐

    (b) Many of the world's resources are nonrenewable. ☐

    (c) Pollution is an environmental issue which only affects people. ☐

2. Name the three types of pollution

    _____

    _____

    _____

3. Name three causes of air pollution.

    _____

    _____

    _____

4. Water pollution occurs when

    _____

    _____

5. Name the three main causes of land pollution.

    _____

    _____

    _____

6. Name the place where domestic waste is dumped.

    _____

✂

Quiz **Deforestation** Pages 24–27

1. Deforestation is _____

    _____

2. As the world's population increases, deforestation occurs in order to:

    (a) _____

    (b) _____

    (c) _____

3. Give two other reasons for deforestation.

    _____

    _____

4. Deforestation results in more _____ in the atmosphere.

5. Trees help to _____ the world's climate.

6. Give four consequences of climate changes as a result of deforestation.

    • _____   • _____

    • _____   • _____

Quiz — Biodiversity

1. Biodiversity means _____

2. The three kinds of biodiversity are …

    (a) _____

    (b) _____

    (c) _____

3. Biodiversity is important because

    _____

    _____

4. Name four natural occurrences which affect biodiversity.

    _____

    _____

    _____

5. What has the main impact on biodiversity?

    _____

    _____

6. Name four different effects humans have had on biodiversity.

    _____

    _____

    _____

    _____

7. One way to preserve biodiversity is

    _____

    _____

Quiz — Conservation

1. List four other aspects of nature that are important to conserve and protect.

    animals, soil, _____

2. Complete the sentence.

    Conservationists aim to put preservation practices in place that have _____ effect on the environment.

3. Name three types of waterways people can pollute.

    _____   _____   _____

4. Write the name of one conservation awareness group.

    _____

5. Name something a government can create to help conserve the environment.

    _____

6. Describe something people can do in each area below to conserve the environment.

    (a) save energy _____

    (b) save gasoline _____

1. Check the classification closest to an animal or plant becoming extinct.

   (a) *vulnerable* ☐   (b) *critically endangered* ☐   (c) *endangered* ☐

2. What is the main reason species are becoming endangered today?

   _____

3. Give two reasons why rainforest areas are particularly at risk of animal and plant species becoming endangered.

   (a) _____

   (b) _____

4. Complete the sentence.

   Animals are _____ or poached for meat, body parts, _____,

   skin, or _____ for pets.

5. State one way introduced species are a threat to native animals.

   _____

6. Add three more examples of pollution that can be a threat to animals and plants.

   chemicals, motor vehicle exhausts, _____

✂

1. Give one example of how we use energy in our daily lives. _____

   _____

2. Check if the energy source is renewable and cross if it nonrenewable.

   (a) natural gas .... ☐   (b) wind .... ☐   (c) uranium .... ☐

   (d) solar .... ☐   (e) coal .... ☐   (f) biomass .... ☐

   (g) geothermal .... ☐   (h) hydropower .... ☐   (i) oil .... ☐

3. What is another name given to non-renewable energy sources?

   _____

4. Why must we be careful about using energy? _____

   _____

5. Next to each word, give an example of how we can conserve energy.

   (a) fridge   _____

   (b) lights   _____

   (c) gasoline   _____

   (d) airconditioning _____

Complete the sentences.

1. Global warming is the general term used to describe _____

   _____

2. Global warming is caused by _____

3. Greenhouse gases are gases which _____

   _____

4. Two greenhouse gases are _____

5. Greenhouse gases are released into the atmosphere by _____

   _____

6. Fossil fuels are mainly used _____

   _____

7. Global warming can cause _____ change.

8. One way to alleviate global warming is to _____

   _____

Answer true or false?

☐ 1. Ozone is made up of two oxygen atoms joined together.

☐ 2. Ozone can be good or bad, depending on its location.

☐ 3. Ozone in the upper atmosphere performs a very valuable task.

☐ 4. Ozone in the lower atmosphere is good for the Earth.

☐ 5. The ozone layer is not really a layer at all.

☐ 6. The ozone layer keeps out harmful UV radiation.

☐ 7. Harmful UV rays can cause skin cancer and cataracts.

☐ 8. The ozone hole is really a "thinning out" of the ozone.

☐ 9. The ozone hole is worse above the Arctic than anywhere else.

☐ 10. The ozone hole above the Antarctic is worse every winter.

☐ 11. The short name for chlorofluorocarbons is CFCs.

☐ 12. CFCs are made when fossil fuels such as gasoline are burned.

☐ 13. Ozone depletion cannot be remedied.

1. Complete the sentence.
   Soil degradation is the name used to describe _____ done to the land
   which reduces its ability to produce _____ agricultural products.

2. Circle the objects which can contribute to soil degradation.
   (a) pesticides ...... ☐   (b) cattle ...... ☐   (c) machinery .... ☐   (d) wind .... ☐
   (e) water .... ☐   (f) salt .... ☐   (g) trees .... ☐   (h) grass .... ☐

3. Check true or false.
   (a) Soils can become harmful to some plants and animals through long-term use of fertilizers and pesticides.   True False
   (b) Compacting soils reduces the space for oxygen around the roots of plants.   True False
   (c) Erosion occurs when ground water close to the surface rises.   True False
   (d) Salty soils are difficult to grow plants in.   True False
   (e) Sheep and cattle can destroy soils.   True False
   (f) The condition of soils has no effect on anyone except farmers.   True False

4. One way to improve soils is by _____

---

1. What is the name of a scientist who genetically modifies food?
   _____

2. What do some rice crops contain to help prevent blindness in poorer Asian countries?
   _____

3. Give one reason why salmon are being farmed that grow three times faster than a wild salmon.
   _____

4. What could food for poultry and livestock contain to boost their immunity?
   _____

5. List two things GM food crops use less of that helps the environment.
   _____
   _____

6. Fill in the missing words about some environmental problems of GM foods.
   (a) Pests may develop _____ to the crops created to kill them.
   (b) GM crops could be _____ to other species in a food chain.
   (c) Unknown _____ could result from the mass production of GM foods.

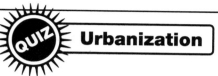 **Urbanization**

1. Write a synonym for each of these.

    (a) rural _____

    (b) urban _____

2. What might the population be of …

    (a) an extremely densely populated urban area?

    _____

    (b) a moderately populated urban area?

    _____

3. List three reasons animal and plant habitats are destroyed.

    (a) _____

    (b) _____

    (c) _____

4. Complete these sentences about urbanization and water pollution.

    (a) In urban areas, water is channelled into _____ systems where it picks up ground

    _____.

    (b) _____ sites are a way of collecting waste disposal and can be a problem if they _____ soil and ground water.

5. List two ways air is polluted in urban areas.

    (a) _____

    (b) _____

Natural Disasters

Pages 64–67

1. Write the correct name of each natural disaster.

    (a) Lack of rainfall over a long period.

    _____

    (b) A storm that forms over the western Pacific Ocean.

    _____

    (c) A monstrous wave.

    _____

    (d) The shaking of the ground.

    _____

    (e) A violent, whirling wind.

    _____

    (f) An overflowing body of water.

    _____

    (g) An eruption of melted rock and gas.

    _____

    (h) A large mass of sliding ice and snow.

    _____

    (i) Strong winds, heavy smoke, showers of embers.

    _____

2. True or false?

    (a) A flood is the most common natural disaster. ☐

    (b) A tsunami can be caused by volcanic eruption. ☐

    (c) A wildfire causes soil erosion. ☐

    (d) A cyclone is an area of high pressure. ☐

©World Teachers Press®   www.worldteacherspress.com   ENVIRONMENTAL ISSUES   15

Quiz — Reduce, Reuse, Recycle

1. What two greenhouse gases does decomposing garbage produce?

   (a) _____

   (b) _____

2. What two elements must be present for garbage to decompose?

   (a) _____

   (b) _____

3. Give a definition of the following:

   (a) Recycling _____

   (b) Reducing _____

   (c) Reusing _____

4. Give four examples of materials which can be:

   (a) Recycled _____

   (b) Reduced _____

   (c) Reused _____

Quiz — Pesticides

1. How do pesticides increase overseas exports of food?

   _____

   _____

   _____

   _____

2. Why are pesticides used in gardens?

   _____

   _____

   _____

   _____

3. What is spray drift?

   _____

   _____

   _____

4. Why is it dangerous to use too much pesticide in gardens?

   _____

   _____

   _____

5. Why are the long-term effects of pesticides of such concern?

   _____

   _____

   _____

6. What should be done about the problem of pesticides?

   _____

   _____

   _____

Quiz Hazardous Waste

1. What can hazardous waste damage?

   _____

   _____

2. Where does hazardous waste come from?

   _____

   _____

3. What is toxic waste?

   _____

   _____

4. Name two substances in your home that become hazardous waste.

   _____

   _____

5. Why are the long-term problems of hazardous waste hard for people to understand?

   _____

   _____

   _____

   _____

   _____

   _____

6. What is a "nontoxic" cleaner?

   _____

   _____

   _____

Quiz Water Resources

1. Why is 2 percent of the Earth's fresh water unavailable for use?

   _____

   _____

2. Is there more fresh water or salt water on the Earth's surface?

   _____

   _____

3. What makes water so vulnerable to pollution?

   _____

   _____

4. How do pesticides and herbicides affect water quality?

   _____

5. What needs to be done to some water to make it suitable for drinking?

   _____

   _____

6. What is most of the Earth's fresh water used for?

   _____

   _____

   _____

7. How can domestic water consumption be reduced?

   _____

   _____

   _____

   _____

Pollution 20–23

1. (a), (b)
2. air, water, land
3. Answers may include: factories, power plants, cars, trucks, buses, chemicals, wood heaters, windblown dust, wildfires
4. Water is contaminated by waste which is dumped or drained into it.
5. Dumping unwanted or untreated waste; littering; disposal of domestic waste.
6. landfill
7. Teacher check

Deforestation 24–27

1. ... the process of clearing land of trees or forests by cutting, burning or by other means in order to use the land for a different purpose.
2. (a) provide land for agriculture
   (b) satisfy the demand for wood and wood products
   (c) build more homes
3. mining, subsistence farming, cattle grazing
4. carbon dioxide
5. regulate
6. soil becomes less productive; soil erosion; higher daytime and cooler nighttime temperatures; changes to the water cycle; loss of plant and animal species; flooding; more deserts

Biodiversity 28–31

1. ... the variety of life on Earth
2. (a) habitat diversity
   (b) species diversity
   (c) genetic diversity
3. ... all living things are interconnected. A change in one area of biodiversity affects another.
4. volcanic eruptions, meteor impacts, glaciers, wildfires, floods, storms, earthquakes
5. humans
6. destroy habitats, change ecosystems, overuse natural resources, expand agriculture and forestry, import nonnative species
7. Answers will include: control pollution, conserve resources, protect endangered species and their habitats, restrict deforestation, find alternative energy sources.

Conservation 32–35

1. plants, water, landscape, air
2. minimal
3. Answers could include: beaches, oceans, rivers, lakes, wetlands
4. Greenpeace, WWF or IUCN
5. National park, reserve, zoo, or wildlife park
6. (a) buying energy-efficent electrical goods, turning off lights, or insulating the home
   (b) riding a bike, walking, or using public transportation

Endangered Species 36–39

1. (b)
2. Humans destroying animals' and plants' habitats.
3. (a) the ecosystem is so delicate
   (b) home to more than half of the world's species
4. hunted/killed, fur, trapped/ caught
5. Answers may include: destroy their habitats, compete for the same food supply or shelter, or prey on the native species.
6. Answers should include three of the following: fertilizers, nuclear waste, factory wastes, spilled oil, plastics in the ocean.

Energy Sources 40–43

1. Teacher check
2. (b), (d), (f), (g) and (h) should be checked; (a), (c), (e) and (i) should be crossed
3. fossil fuels
4. Nonrenewable energy sources will eventually all be used up.
5. Teacher check

Global Warming 44–47

1. ... an average increase in the temperature of the Earth.
2. human activity
3. ... trap heat from the sun and prevent it going back out into space
4. carbon dioxide, nitrous oxide, or methane

5. fossils fuels such as coal, oil and gas
6. ... to produce electricity for homes and industry; for oil for cars, trucks, etc.
7. climate
8. Answers will vary but should include reusing, recycling resources, using alternate power sources, planting trees, taking care of the environment, etc.

Ozone Depletion 48–51

1. False   8. True
2. True   9. False
3. True   10. False
4. False   11. True
5. True   12. False
6. True   13. False
7. True

Soil Degradation 52–55

1. damage, quality
2. (a), (b), (c), (d), (e), (f)
3. (a) True (b) True
   (c) False (d) True
   (e) True (f) False
4. Teacher check

Genetically-Modified Foods 56–59

1. genetic engineer
2. Vitamin A
3. helping with overfishing/ cheaper to produce
4. vaccines
5. water/fertilizer/pesticides
6. (a) resistance
   (b) harmful
   (c) viruses

Urbanization 60–63

1. (a) country
   (b) city/town
2. Teacher check
   (a) possibly hundreds of thousands or millions
   (b) possibly a few thousand
3. Answers could include: for roads, for residential areas, for industries, for recreational areas.
4. (a) run-off, pollutants/contaminants
   (b) Landfill, contaminate/pollute
5. Answers could include: motor vehicle exhausts, gases and chemicals from industry, smoke from wood heaters.

Natural Disasters 64–67

1. (a) drought
   (b) typhoon
   (c) tsunami
   (d) earthquake
   (e) tornado
   (f) flood
   (g) volcano
   (h) avalanche
   (i) wildfire
2. (a) true   (b) true
   (c) false   (d) false

Reduce, Reuse, Recycle 68–71

1. (a) carbon dioxide
   (b) methane
2. (a) water
   (b) oxygen
3. (a) Recycling means to turn a waste product into the same product or something different so that it can be used again.
   (b) Reducing means buying and using fewer products which create waste.
   (c) Reusing means to use the same item many times instead of discarding it after one use.
4. Answers may include:
   (a) glass, metal, paper, aluminum, plastics, acid batteries, building materials, chemicals, electronic equipment, lead, oil, paint, tires, white goods
   (b) packaging, plastic bags, junk mail, water, etc.
   (c) boxes, plastic containers, newspapers, toys, clothing, bottles, jars, etc.
5. Teacher check

Pesticides 72–75

1. They improve the quantity and quality of the food produced.
2. They are used to kill weeds or insects that destroy plants.
3. Sprayed chemicals are spread beyond the intended area, usually by wind.
4. The pesticide can be washed into waterways, where it can destroy aquatic life, or into the soil, where it may affect small creatures and can contaminate drinking water.
5. They are hard to detect so some people don't know or want to know about them.
6. research and education

Hazardous Waste 76–79

1. It can cause damage to the environment and to health.
2. It can come from many sources, including businesses, industry and our homes.
3. It is waste that is poisonous and can cause death or injury.
4. Answers will vary.
5. They can't see or believe the danger because it takes a long time to become obvious.
6. It is a cleaner that is not harmful to people or the environment.

Water Resources.....80–83

1. It is frozen in the polar ice caps and in glaciers.
2. salt
3. It is an excellent solvent.
4. They pollute waterways, particularly ground water, when there is insufficient soil to filter them. They come from domestic and agricultural sources.
5. It needs to be filtered, boiled, or have chemicals like chlorine added.
6. It is used in agriculture, particularly irrigation, to produce food.
7. Answers may include: more efficient appliances, less water-hungry gardens, detection of leaks and increasing consumer costs.

Pollution

Indicators

- *Reads information and answers questions about pollution.*
- *Completes poetry about pollution, using a given framework.*

Worksheet Information

- Air pollution can include domestic smoke, smog and industrial pollutants. It can lead to acid rain, the greenhouse effect and depletion of the Earth's ozone layer. It is estimated that over a third of all the smoke in the atmosphere is produced in people's homes from coal fires.
- Smog was given its name because it looked like a mixture of **sm**oke and f**og**. It is made up of particles which are triggered into forming by sunlight. Smog is most prevalent in urban areas, where there are a lot of transportation vehicles.
- Students should write generalizations to answer Question 4 on page 22, such as those given in the final paragraph on page 21.
- Review various poetry formats before allowing students to select their own to answer Question 3 on page 23.
- Quiz questions relating to this section may be found on page 10.

Answers

page 22

1. Answers will vary but should mention that Earth's resources are nonrenewable.
2. air, water, land
3. Teacher check
4. Teacher check

page 23

Teacher check

Cross-Curricular Activities

- Students write arguments "for" and "against" a debate about the use of fossil fuels in industry.
- Students conduct experiments using oil on water in a container and various types of materials for cleaning up "polluted waters."
- Students read accounts of a major oil spill from a tanker, such as the *Exxon Valdez* spill, and investigate how this affected the birds, animals and environment.

Many of the world's natural resources are nonrenewable. Human beings are the only inhabitants of the Earth who have the ability to care for or destroy these natural resources. Unfortunately, all too often, human beings have used resources without regard for the impact they are having. As a result, many environmental issues have arisen which need to be addressed for the benefit of the Earth and its inhabitants. One of these is pollution.

Pollution is "any change affecting the environment which makes it harmful to living things." Both humans and animals can be affected by pollution.

The three main types of pollution are air, water and land pollution.

Air pollution comes from sources such as factories, power plants, cars, trucks, buses, chemicals, wood heaters, windblown dust and wildfires. It affects the health of human beings, causing breathing difficulties, sore eyes, sore throats and allergies. Air pollution can kill trees and animals and affect lakes and crops. It can cause the ozone layer to thin, letting in more damaging ultraviolet rays from the sun. It can also damage buildings and artistic or historical structures. Fortunately, air pollution can be improved, such as by the use of cleaner sources of power, alternative or more efficient use of transportation, reducing the use of certain chemicals for industrial and domestic use and restricting the use of household wood heaters.

Water covers 70 percent of the Earth, with only 3 percent of this being fresh water. **Water pollution** occurs when water is contaminated by waste which is dumped or drained into it. Sewage (human waste and waste water), chemical waste from factories, oil spills and runoff from agricultural areas are the main sources of water pollution. Pollution can affect the availability of water for household use, the use of rivers, lakes and oceans for recreational purposes, fishing, transportation, industry and delicate water ecosystems. Water pollution can be minimized by treating waste water from homes and factories before it is released back into waterways, controlling the quantity of waste released, by treating waste water for reuse in agriculture or industry, and by humans exercising greater caution so that oil and other pollutants do not enter waterways.

Land pollution is the direct result of three main actions — dumping unwanted or untreated waste products on the land, littering, and disposing of domestic waste. As the world population increases, more and more bottles, cans and packaging are discarded daily. The results of this are mountains of rubbish in landfill areas, unpleasant smells and breeding grounds for pests such as rats and mice. All of these can lead to health problems.

Other causes of land pollution include clearing of land for construction of houses, shops, or roads, and overuse of the land through intensive farming practices such as large-scale grazing of animals and crop growing. This creates poor soils which are easily eroded by wind and rain.

By becoming more aware of the environmental problems, using some creative thinking, and through commitment and the willingness to modify lifestyles, these problems may be alleviated.

Pollution - 2

Use the text on page 21 to answer the questions.

1. Why do we need to look after the Earth's natural resources?

    _____

    _____

2. The three main types of pollution are _____

3. Complete the table for each type of pollution.

	Main Cause	**Some Effects**	**Possible Solutions**
_____ pollution			
_____ pollution			
_____ pollution			

4. In your own opinion what is the best way to solve all of these problems?

    _____

    _____

Fact File

*Noise pollution can cause stress, which may lead to illness. It is measured in decibel units.
Each ten-decibel increase represents a tenfold increase in noise intensity.*

A cinquain is a poem consisting of five lines and which describes something. It follows this format:

Line 1 — one word or two syllables describe the topic
Line 2 — two words or four syllables describe the title
Line 3 — three words or six syllables describe what the topic does
Line 4 — four words or eight syllables describe the feeling or mood
Line 5 — one word or two syllables with a meaning similar to the topic

1. Read the cinquain about pollution.

> **Pollution**
> **Foul, menacing**
> **Destroying, choking, changing**
> **Worrying, urging, cautioning, alarming**
> **Unclean**

2. Use the following formats to write pollution poetry.

   (a) A *haiku* is made up of three lines:

   Line 1 — has five syllables and states "where it is."
   Line 2 — has seven syllables and states "what it is" or "what it is doing."
   Line 3 — has five syllables and states "when or what is being felt" or "what is happening."

   _____

   _____

   _____

   (b) A *string poem* describes a keyword.

   Line 1 — the key word is written three times
   Line 2 — gives a visual description
   Line 3 — describes the size
   Line 4 — describes what it does
   Line 5 — describes something interesting
   Line 6 — the key word is written three times

   > 3. Select a poetry format of your own to write a pollution poem on a separate sheet of paper.

   _____

   _____

   _____

   _____

   _____

Fact File

Acid rain is one result of air pollution. It is caused when rain becomes acidic as gases dissolve in rainwater. These gases are produced mainly by burning fossil fuels in power stations and by using them in vehicles.

Deforestation

Indicators

- *Reads information and answers questions about deforestation.*
- *Completes a word search using topic word clues.*

Worksheet Information

- Teachers may wish to discuss in more detail the causes and effects of, and suggested solutions to, deforestation.
- Quiz questions relating to this section may be found on page 10.

Answers

page 26

1. Teacher check
2. Answers will vary, but should include agricultural use, cattle grazing, demand for wood products, commercial logging, urban sprawl, mining and subsistence farming.
3. Atmospheric changes, climate change; Teacher check
4. Teacher check

page 27

1. deforestation
2. population
3. mining, logging, cattle grazing
4. wood products
5. urbanization
6. carbon dioxide, oxygen
7. subsistence
8. climate change
9. clearing trees
10. alternative, replanting, education, controls

Cross-Curricular Activities

- Students draw diagrams which illustrate the effect of deforestation on the climate.
- Students write a fictional story about an animal which lost its habitat due to deforestation.
- Students collect and collate figures which show the rate of deforestation in specific areas, such as the Amazon or Daintree Rainforests.

Deforestation is the process of clearing the land of trees or forests by cutting, burning or by other means in order to use the land for a different purpose.

As the world's population continues to increase, deforestation occurs in order to:

- Provide more land for agricultural use to obtain needed products. Large plantations supply foods such as fruit, vegetables, nuts, spices, coffee, chocolate and sugar. Large areas of land must be cleared to provide grazing land for beef and dairy cattle or for growing cereal crops. Other products include ingredients for medicines and chewing gum, chemicals to make perfumes, cosmetics, soap, shampoo, disinfectants, detergents and polishes, and materials to make rope and baskets.

- Satisfy the demand for wood for firewood and wood products for building. Logging companies build dams and roads for transporting timber such as mahogany, teak, rosewood and other hardwoods. Commercial logging employs the use of heavy machinery such as bulldozers and road graders to level trees in huge quantities and provide access to timber.

- Allow towns and cities to continue to grow by clearing land to build new homes for people to live in.

Mining for materials such as iron, manganese, bauxite, gold, copper and nickel also require large areas of land to be cleared.

Some farmers clear the land to grow crops for their own use. These are called subsistence farmers. The soils where they farm are usually very poor and so cannot be used more than once. Each year, subsistence farmers clear new areas of land to grow crops to feed their families.

Deforestation can have many detrimental effects. The most obvious of these is as a result of the fact that trees take in carbon dioxide and give out oxygen. Carbon dioxide in the atmosphere —from industry and transportation—increases because there are not as many trees to convert the carbon dioxide to oxygen. This may lead to a rise in global temperature. Plants, animals and humans can all be affected.

Trees help cool and regulate the world's climate. As more trees are destroyed, changes to climate may result in:

- dryer, less productive soils and more soil erosion,
- higher temperatures during the day and cooler temperatures at night,
- changes to the water cycle as less water is being retained,
- the loss of many plant and animal species,
- increased flooding,
- expanding desert areas.

Since there are many causes of deforestation, there must be a number of solutions. Some may take many years to be effective. Finding alternative products to use instead of those taken from forests, using farming land better, replanting lost trees, educating people about the problem of deforestation and stricter controls for using forest areas are some solutions to consider.

Use the text on page 25 to answer the questions.

1. Write a definition of deforestation.

_____

_____

_____

2. Give five reasons to explain why deforestation occurs.

• _____

• _____

• _____

• _____

• _____

3. Make notes about some of the detrimental effects of deforestation.

4. Next to each cause of deforestation, suggest a solution from the text or an idea of your own.

(a) large-scale agricultural use _____

(b) cattle grazing _____

(c) high demand for wood products _____

(d) commercial logging _____

(e) "urban sprawl" _____

(f) mining _____

(g) subsistence farming _____

Fact File

Carbon dioxide is called a greenhouse gas because it acts like the glass in a greenhouse.
It lets in heat from the sun and then traps it in the atmosphere!

Use the clues to find words in the word search.

c	a	r	b	o	n	d	i	o	x	i	d	e	c
a	n	s	l	o	g	g	i	n	g	s	o	k	l
t	o	y	e	f	j	c	a	p	o	t	c	x	i
t	i	s	s	b	t	l	e	b	c	c	n	d	m
l	t	u	a	r	q	e	v	u	o	u	r	w	a
e	a	b	n	u	c	a	i	p	n	d	e	p	t
g	z	s	o	v	s	r	t	d	t	o	p	o	e
r	i	i	i	x	o	i	a	r	r	r	l	p	c
a	n	s	t	d	y	n	n	g	o	p	a	u	h
z	a	t	a	w	e	g	r	n	l	d	n	l	a
i	b	e	c	f	x	t	e	i	s	o	t	a	n
n	r	n	u	t	v	r	t	n	k	o	i	t	g
g	u	c	d	y	g	e	l	i	i	w	n	i	e
m	n	e	e	n	z	e	a	m	d	j	g	o	l
d	e	f	o	r	e	s	t	a	t	i	o	n	m

Fact File

"Slash and burn" is a very common way for small farmers to clear land for farming. A few acres of trees are slashed down and the remaining tree trunks are burned away!

1. The name given to the process of clearing trees. _____

2. An increase in this means more houses need to be built. _____

3. Three industries which land is cleared for.

   _____   _____   _____

4. Trees are logged to obtain these. _____

5. The spread of towns and cities. _____

6. Trees take in _____ and give out _____.

7. The name for a type of farming where crops are grown to feed the farmer and not for sale.

   _____

8. Trees help to prevent _____ around the world.

9. Deforestation is the process of _____.

10. Some solutions to deforestation include using _____ products,

    better land management, _____ trees, _____,

    stricter _____ of tree clearing.

Indicators

- *Reads information and answers questions about biodiversity.*
- *Completes information about a variety of species.*

Worksheet Information

- The following Web sites provide information about the classifications given:

    http://encyclopedia.worldvillage.com/s/b/Scientific_classification#Human_.28Homo_sapiens.29

    http://en.wikipedia.org/wiki/Japanese_beetle

- Students may need to be prompted with familiar words to help them to answer questions on page 31; for example, Insecta and Scarabaeidae may need explanations..

- Quiz questions relating to this section may be found on page 11.

Answers

page 30

1. Teacher check
2. habitat diversity, species diversity, genetic diversity
3. Teacher check
4. Teacher check
5. controlling pollution, conserving resources, protecting endangered species and their habitat, restricting deforestation, finding alternate sources of energy

page 31

1. (a) human beings
   (b) Japanese beetle
2. (a) Kingdom – Animalia; Phylum – Arthropoda; Class – Insecta; Order – Diptera
   (b) Kingdom – Plantae; Division – Magnoliophyta; Class – Magnoliopsida; Order – Asterales; Family – Asteraceae
3. (a) smelly house dog
   (b) small, white bird
   (c) large, green tree
   (d) clear, fluffy clouds
   (e) Teacher check

Cross-Curricular Activities

- Students investigate words which come from the same Greek or Latin source; for example, biology, biography, biosphere.
- Students research to create a chart which explains where each of their own physical characteristics, mannerisms or talents may have come from; e.g., blue eyes from father.
- Students complete a profile of a plant or animal which has evolved into a large number of species; e.g., ants, roses.

What is biodiversity?

"bio"—life; "diversity"—variety

Biodiversity is the name given to describe the variety of life on Earth. It includes all plants, animals and microorganisms, as well as the many different varieties within each species and the ecosystems they live in.

There are three kinds of biodiversity—habitat diversity, species diversity and genetic diversity.

- Habitat (or ecosystem) diversity includes the many different habitats, biological communities and natural systems in which plants and animals live. It includes ecosystems such as savannas, rainforests, oceans, marshes, deserts and any other environment in which a species may live.

- Species diversity refers to the variety of living species. Some estimates suggest that there are between 1.5 and 1.7 million named species on Earth, including insects, plants, fish, reptiles and amphibians, birds, mammals, mollusks, worms, spiders, fungi, algae and microorganisms. There may be millions more which have not been identified.

- Genetic diversity refers to the variety of genetic characteristics found within a particular species and among different species. Plants and animals may have thousands of genes, providing huge varieties within one species. Humans differ by many physical aspects including hair, eye and skin color and in the way they live. A visit to a supermarket shows many different varieties of the same fruit or vegetable.

Why is biodiversity important?

Everything on Earth forms part of the web of life, including humans. Plants regulate the air we breathe, provide food and medicines, and remove greenhouse gases, particularly carbon dioxide, from the atmosphere. Insects, worms and bacteria break down wastes and help to decompose dead plants and animals to enrich soils. All living things are interconnected. A change in one area of biodiversity affects another.

How is biodiversity being affected?

The Earth's biodiversity is constantly changing. A number of things affect biodiversity, including natural events such as volcanic eruptions, meteor impacts, glaciers, wildfires, floods, storms, or earthquakes. Humans have the greatest impact on biodiversity. They destroy habitats; change delicate ecosystems by polluting the air, soil and water; overuse plants and animals for food, medicines, and raw materials for industry; expand agriculture and forestry industries; and even import nonnative species into unsuitable environments.

What can we do to preserve biodiversity?

The preservation of the variety of plants and animals on Earth is very complex and requires a number of solutions. Some of those solutions may include controlling pollution; conserving resources; protecting endangered species and their habitats; restricting deforestation; and finding alternative sources of energy for domestic and industrial use. Whatever solutions are chosen must be balanced carefully against satisfying basic human needs. We live in a beautiful world. Future generations should be able to enjoy it as well!

Biodiversity - 2

Use the text on page 29 to answer the questions.

1. In your own words, write a definition of "biodiversity."

   _____

   _____

2. The three kinds of biodiversity are:

3. Write an explanation of each type of biodiversity.

   (a) _____

   _____

   (b) _____

   _____

   (c) _____

   _____

4. Draw a diagram or flow chart which explains why biodiversity is important.

5. List some ways to preserve biodiversity.

   _____

   _____

   _____

   Fact File

   Scientists believe that there are millions of species, including microorganisms and invertebrates such as worms and insects, undiscovered.

Species Classifications

Scientists classify a species using a variety of specific group and subgroup names.

1. Read the following classifications and state which species is being described.

(a)

Kingdom	Animalia
Phylum	Chordata (has a backbone)
Class	Mammalia (nurses its young)
Order	Primates
Family	Hominidae
Genus	Homo
Species	Sapiens

The species is _____

(b)

Kingdom	Animalia
Phylum	Arthropoda
Class	Insecta
Order	Coleoptera
Family	Scarabaeidae
Genus	Popillia
Species	P. japonica

The species is _____

2. Use the following Web sites to complete the classifications for the species below.

http://en.wikipedia.org/wiki/Dandelion
http://encyclopedia.worldvillage.com/s/b/Scientific_classification#Human_.28homosapiens.29

fruit fly	
Kingdom	
Phylum	
Class	
Order	
Family	Drosophilidae
Genus	Drosophila
Species	D. melanogaster

common dandelion	
Kingdom	
Division	
Class	
Order	
Family	
Genus	Taraxacum
Species	Taraxacum officinale

Often a species is given a Latin name to help identify it. For example, the common housefly is *Musca domestica* and the honeybee is *Apis mellifera*.

3. Write what these "made-up" Latin names may be describing and make up one of your own.

(a) od domestica caninus   _____

(b) minimus albinus avia   _____

(c) gigantus greenis arbora   _____

(d) transparentia downius cirrus   _____

(e) _____   _____

Fact File

Tropical rainforests are the home for from 50 to 90 percent of all species on Earth!

Conservation

Indicators

- *Reads information and answers questions about the importance of conservation.*
- *Creates a billboard outlining appropriate rules in a national park.*

Worksheet Information

- Although conservation includes the protection of historic buildings, only natural things are discussed since this topic deals with environmental issues.

- The billboard students are asked to create on page 35 can be for an imaginary or an actual national park. Students could use a search engine on the Internet and type in the name of a known national park or key words such as "national park rules" to assist them.

- Quiz questions relating to this section can be found on page 11.

Answers

page 34

1. protection, careful, natural

2. Conservationists promote the preservation of significant areas in their natural state by putting practices in place which result in minimal impact on the environment.

3–5. Teacher check

page 35

Teacher check

Cross-Curricular Activities

- Brainstorm to list ways students can conserve the environment at school, within their classroom and or the school grounds. Extend to students' homes and families.

- Hold a discussion or debate about whether tourism should be stopped in national parks.

- Record and photograph or sketch the names of the plants and animals that live in a park or natural area near the school. Care should be taken not to disturb any wildlife.

Conservation is the protection of nature or historic buildings and the careful use of natural things. This includes fauna (animals), flora (plants), water (oceans, rivers, lakes, wetlands, etc.), soil, the landscape, air and other natural resources. Conservationists are people who promote the preservation of areas which are significant—scientifically or culturally—in their natural state. They aim to do this by putting practices in place which result in minimal impact on the environment. Our environment is our most valuable resource, as it holds the key to our survival.

Conserving the environment is extremely important today, as people have had an impact on it to such an extent that the damage will take years to repair—some damage may not be able to be repaired at all. Some of the ways people have damaged the environment are:

- littering public places, including recreational areas and nature reserves
- polluting waterways, including beaches, the wider ocean, rivers, lakes and wetlands
- using up nonrenewable resources such as coal, oil and gas
- destroying native vegetation to make way for roads, residential, and industrial areas, thereby threatening native animals and plants
- farming methods which have led to areas known as "dust bowls," as well as increased salt in the soil, resulting in land useless for animals, plants and people
- overusing water supplies
- polluting the atmosphere, which directly affects people's health.

There are many ways people and governments can conserve the environment. Some of these are explained below.

1. National parks and reserves, both land and marine, protect the environment, yet still allow people to see and enjoy the natural beauty. Each national park has specific rules visitors must follow, such as not feeding the animals, not disturbing or removing the animals and plants, and driving only on designated roads.

2. Groups such as the World Conservation Union (IUCN), Greenpeace and the WWF (formerly the World Wildlife Fund) aim to build awareness of environmental issues and to make sure environmental rules are followed by people, governments and industries.

3. Zoos and wildlife parks incorporate captive breeding programs for particular threatened and endangered species. They also aim to inform and educate people about these issues and to involve them in conservation.

4. People can change their lifestyles to meet the needs of the environment and lessen the negative impact on it. Some of these changes include:

   - Saving energy by buying energy-efficient electrical goods, turning off unnecessary lights and insulating the home.
   - Saving water by fixing leaking faucets and following garden watering restrictions.
   - Riding a bike, walking or using public transportation to save nonrenewable gasoline.
   - Recycling waste such as glass, aluminum, plastics and newspapers.
   - Donating blankets, furniture and unwanted clothes to charity organizations.

Use the text on page 33 to answer the questions.

1. Complete the sentence to define "conservation."

   Conservation is the _____ of nature and historic

   buildings and the _____ use of _____ things.

2. Describe the job of conservationists and how they aim to achieve it.

   _____

   _____

   _____

3. List four ways people have had an impact on the environment.

   _____

   _____

   _____

   _____

4. Use key words and phrases to explain how the environment is conserved under each heading.

National Parks And Reserves	Conservation Groups	Zoos and Wildlife Parks

5. List four ways you can change your lifestyle to lessen your impact on the environment.

   _____

   _____

   _____

   _____

Fact File

The conservation group Greenpeace has offices in about 30 countries worldwide and has 2.5 million members.

National Park Billboard

Creating national parks is one way governments can protect and conserve the environment, while still allowing people to see and enjoy its natural beauty. However, each park has special rules for visitors to follow. Many of these are common to all parks, while others relate only to a particular national park.

1. Create a billboard to erect at a national park to inform visitors about the rules they must follow. Use nonfiction resources, such as the Internet, to help you make a list of rules. You will need to consider the following:

    - Type of national park
    - Rules for personal behavior
    - Use of vehicles in the park
    - Rules to follow to protect the environment
    - Recreational activities permitted
    - Safety precautions

Welcome to _____ National Park

Fact File

In 1872, Yellowstone National Park in the United States became the world's first national park. It covers an area of about 2,219,799 acres and includes parts of the states of Wyoming, Montana and Idaho.

Endangered Species

Indicators

- *Reads information and answers questions about endangered species.*
- *Researches to write a report on an endangered animal or plant.*

Worksheet Information

- The IUCN (World Conservation Union) has status categories for listing threatened plant and animal species as shown at right:

  These categories allow for greater understanding of the urgency level and action required for threatened species.

- Students may need a dictionary to complete Question 1 on page 38.

- Quiz questions relating to this section can be found on page 12.

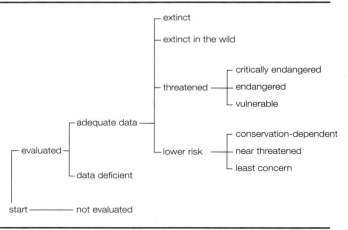

Answers

page 38

1. (a) to be in danger or at risk
   (b) to be in possible danger
   (c) not strong or protected
   (d) severely

2. Many species cannot survive when their habitat is destroyed and they are forced to compete with others for space for a new habitat and food.

3. They are still hunted or poached for meat, body parts, fur, skins, or for pets.

4. (a) they destroy their habitats
   (b) compete for the same food supply and shelter
   (c) they hunt the native species

5. Possible answers could include:
   (a) What do humans use animal and plant habitats for?
   (b) What are some of the types of pollution that affect plants and animal species?
   (c) What are groups such as the IUCN and WWF doing to help conserve endangered and threatened species?

6. A reintroduction program is one where a captive-bred animal is returned to the wild. A relocation program is one where an animal is shifted to a new habitat.

page 39

Teacher check

Cross-Curricular Activities

- Compile lists of animals and plants under the headings "Critically Endangered," "Endangered" and "Vulnerable."

- Discover if any plants or animals in the local area are endangered and what is being done or could be done about the situation.

- Investigate why certain animals' body parts are prized; e.g., elephants' tusks for ivory, snow leopards' white fur, tigers' body parts used in traditional Asian medicines.

A threatened or endangered species is any animal or plant whose numbers are declining to such an extent that it is at risk of disappearing altogether, i.e., becoming extinct. The species can be classified as being critically endangered, endangered or vulnerable, depending on its numbers.

In the past, plants and animals became endangered through natural means, such as when the Earth's climate changed in the Ice Age. Today, species are becoming endangered at an alarming rate due to human interference. Sometimes it is due to one factor, but generally it is a combination of factors. Some of the major reasons are as follows.

Habitat Destruction

This is by far the greatest threat. Increased population growth and industrialization has led to the need for more housing, factories for industry, roads, and farmland for food crops and animal products. Huge areas of land are cleared, along with the animals' and plants' habitats. Many species cannot survive when they are forced to try to adapt to another area and have to compete with others for space for a new habitat and food. Rainforest areas of the world are particularly at risk, as their ecosystem is so delicate. They are also home to more than half of the world's animal and plant species.

Hunting Exploitation

Many animals were, and still are, hunted or poached (illegally hunted) for meat, body parts, fur and skins, or trapped for pets. Overfishing for increased profit causes huge populations of the target fish, and others caught in the nets, to be killed.

Introduced Species

An introduced species is one that is not native to a particular geographic area. Humans have introduced animal and plant species into new environments, either accidentally or as an extra source of food or means of transportation, to solve an environmental problem, or as pets.

These species become a threat to native animals by destroying their habitats, competing for the same food supply and shelter, and even hunting the native species.

Pollution

Over the past 200 years in particular, pollutants such as chemicals, fertilizers, pesticides, nuclear waste, factory wastes, spilled oil, motor vehicle exhaust gases, and plastics in the ocean have seriously affected a large number of terrestrial and marine plants and animals.

How Can The Problem Be Solved?

Groups such as the IUCN (World Conservation Union) and WWF are committed to conserving endangered and threatened species through conducting research, education for both governments and the public, captive breeding programs, reintroduction programs, relocation programs, preservation of natural habitats, and the setting up of animal and plant reserves.

As members of the public, we can support these groups and be aware of the effects of human activities on endangered species.

Use the text on page 37 to answer the questions.

1. Match the definitions for each word.

    (a) endangered •   • not strong or protected
    (b) threatened •   • to be in danger or at risk
    (c) vulnerable •   • severely
    (d) critically •   • to be in possible danger

    Fact File

    Today about 5,500 animal species and as many as half the world's plant species are threatened with extinction.

2. Why is habitat destruction the greatest threat to animal and plant species?

    _____

    _____

    _____

3. Why are many animals still hunted or poached?

    _____

    _____

4. List three ways introduced species have threatened native species.

    (a) _____

    (b) _____

    (c) _____

5. Write a question for these answers.

    (a) Housing, factories for industry, roads and farmland.

    _____

    (b) Chemicals, fertilizers, pesticides, factory wastes and spilled oil.

    _____

    (c) Conducting research, educating the public and governments, captive breeding programs and preserving natural habitats.

    _____

    _____

6. What do you think the difference is between a reintroduction program and a relocation program?

    _____

    _____

Endangered Species Report

It is frightening to think that there are hundreds of animal and plant species under threat of extinction. This includes all types of animals and plants—mammals, birds, fish, insects, reptiles, lilies, vines, palms and mosses, to name just a few.

1. Read through the lists of endangered or vulnerable species below. Choose one of these or one of your own choice to write a report, using suitable resources from the library or the Internet.

Mammals –	snow leopard, orangutan, pygmy hippopotamus, dugong, koala, vicuna
Birds –	kiwi, scarlet macaw, barn owl, Hawaiian goose, black-footed albatross
Reptiles –	tuatara, Nile crocodile, Komodo dragon, Asian cobra, green sea turtle
Insects –	Queen Alexandra's birdwing butterfly, robber fly, basking damselfly
Plants –	Brazilian cactus, Venus flytrap, cucumber tree, alerce tree, St. Helena ebony
Others –	largetooth sawfish, spotted salamander, basking shark, slender seahorse

Endangered Species

Location(s)

Sketch	**Interesting Facts**

Threats to Its Survival

Possible Solutions

Fact File

More than 300,000 of the Earth's estimated 10 million species have become extinct over the past 50 years.

Indicators

- *Reads information and answers questions about energy sources and saving energy.*
- *Conducts an experiment to investigate the insulating properties of various materials.*

Worksheet Information

- Biomass may be an unfamiliar energy source (mentioned on page 41). Biomass energy is made by changing agricultural wastes, trees, grasses, aquatic plants and other organic matter into energy by burning it, changing it to a gas, or converting it to a liquid fuel.

- The materials the students choose for the experiment should be able to be wrapped around the jars as snugly as possible with an elastic band or tape. Students could practice carrying out the experiment without the water to become as efficient as possible, so that time is not a factor with the water temperature cooling down at different rates. The kettle could be reboiled before adding the water to the next jar.

- Students could try the experiment again, leaving the jars for longer or shorter times before measuring the water temperature. What materials insulate better? Is there a time after which none of the materials keeps the jars warm?

- Quiz questions relating to this section can be found on page 12.

Answers

page 42

1. Answers may vary.

2. (a) Renewable energy can be used repeatedly and cannot be used up.

    (b) Nonrenewable energy cannot be replaced or remade once it is used up.

3. A fossil fuel is one that was formed millions of years ago from the fossilized remains of plants and animals.

4. solar power, wind power, hydropower, thermal power, biomass

5. (a) appliances, not

    (b) insulation, walls, reduce, heat

    (c) rating

    (d) shorter, unnecessary

    (e) car pool, public

    (f) door, seal

6. Teacher check

page 43

Teacher check

Cross-Curricular Activities

- Investigate the problems associated with renewable energy development; e.g., bird deaths when they collide with the wind turbines and wires on wind farms and potential erosion in desert areas from wind farms.

- Compare their families' electricity and gas bills before and after energy-saving practices, or compare between summer and winter.

- Construct and carry out a survey of common appliances at home and school, what form of energy each needs to operate and what each is used for.

Energy is defined as "the ability to do work." Our bodies need energy, through food, for us to do work. We use energy to make things work for us; e.g., energy in the form of electricity to give us light or cook us food, and energy in the form of fossil fuels to drive a car or public transportation.

Energy sources come in different forms—light (radiant), heat (thermal), chemical, electrical, mechanical and nuclear. They are divided into two types, renewable and nonrenewable.

- A *renewable energy source* is one that can be used repeatedly and cannot be used up.

- A *nonrenewable energy source* is one that can not be replaced or remade once it has been used up.

Renewable energy sources – solar (from the sun), wind, hydropower (from water), geothermal (steam from inside the Earth) and biomass (from plants).

Non-renewable energy sources – coal, oil, natural gas and uranium (to make nuclear power). Coal, oil and natural gas are called fossil fuels because they were formed millions of years ago from layers of fossilized plants and animals. Those layers gradually formed a black rock-like substance called coal, a thick liquid called oil, and natural gas.

The main energy we use in our homes, work, factories, schools, etc., is electricity. Fossil fuels are widely used to create electricity, as they are relatively cheap to process. The problem is, however, that fossil fuels are nonrenewable and we will run out of them in the future. We must look to alternative renewable energy sources, including solar, wind, hydro or thermal power and biomass.

Saving Energy

In our modern society, we cannot function without energy, particularly electricity. It is important that we make thoughtful choices about how we can use less energy, and in so doing, conserve our fossil fuels. Some means of conserving energy are outlined below.

- Turn off appliances such as the TV and computers when no one is using them.

- Don't leave unnecessary lights on. The use of fluorescent light bulbs also saves electricity.

- Walk, ride a bike, car pool or use public transportation to save fuel.

- Install insulation in the walls and ceiling space of homes and buildings to reduce the amount of energy needed to cool and heat the living and working areas.

- Wear warm clothing in the house in cold weather before deciding if heating needs to be turned on or up.

- Choose energy-efficient appliances—look for the energy rating.

- Take shorter showers and don't use hot water unnecessarily—this will reduce the energy used to heat the water.

- Don't open the fridge door longer than necessary and it won't use as much energy to keep the inside cold. Make sure the door is closed properly and the seal is still effective.

Energy Sources - 2

Use the text on page 41 to answer the questions.

1. Give two examples of how we use energy to make things work for us.

   (a) _____

   (b) _____

2. Write a definition for these terms.

(a) Renewable energy	(b) Nonrenewable energy

3. What is a fossil fuel?

   _____

   _____

4. List five renewable energy sources.

   _____   _____

   _____   _____

   _____

5. Fill in the missing words about ways we can save energy.

   (a) Turn off _____ such as the TV or computers when _____ in use.

   (b) Install _____ in the ceiling space and _____ of buildings to _____ the amount of energy needed to cool and _____.

   (c) Look for an energy-efficient _____ when choosing a new appliance.

   (d) Take _____ showers and turn off _____ lights.

   (e) Walk, ride a bike, _____ or use _____ public transportation to save gasoline.

   (f) Make sure the fridge _____ is closed properly and the _____ is still effective.

6. Give another example of how you can save energy at home or school.

   _____

   _____

> **Fact File**
>
> *Biomass includes organic matter such as grasses, trees, bark, sawdust, aquatic plants, agricultural waste, and even sewage!*

ENVIRONMENTAL ISSUES ©World Teachers Press® www.worldteacherspress.com

Insulation Experiment

One of the ways we can save energy is by insulating our homes and other buildings. By completing this experiment, you will discover that some materials are better insulators than others. Although you may not be able to test the materials manufacturers use, your results will show you which materials will keep your body warmer in cold weather and cooler in hot weather.

The experiment will be more successful if you work in a group of four.

You will need:
- *identical glass jars with lids (e.g. baby food jars), one for each material you will be testing*
- *kettle*
- *a thermometer*
- *elastic bands and adhesive tape*
- *materials to test suggestions: aluminum foil, cotton, cotton sock, woolen sock, plastic foam, sheet of paper, leather, fiberglass insulation material, cardboard, felt, polyester, rubber, flannel, piece of carpet, plastic bag*

Method:

1. Prepare the materials so they will fit around the jars.

2. Assign each person a job—one to pour hot water from the kettle; one to test the water temperature; one to screw on the lid; and one to wrap the material around the jars, secure and place on the tray.

3. Commence the experiment, one jar at a time, with each person doing his or her job as quickly as possible, so water temperatures are as similar as possible.

4. Pour in water that has recently boiled, measure and record the temperature, screw on the lid, wrap and secure the material with an elastic band or tape and place on a tray in order of first to last done. Leave one jar uncovered as a control.

5. After a specific period of time, e.g., 30 minutes, take off the materials in the order in which they were applied, recording the water temperature each time.

Results:

Material Used	Water Temperature Before Covering	Water Temperature After _____ Minutes/Hours
Control		

Fact File

Although natural gas is odorless, leaks can be detected as it has an organic compound added to it to give it an odor.

Indicators

- *Reads information and answers questions about global warming.*
- *Completes a table to suggest methods to alleviate global warming.*

Worksheet Information

- Discuss in more detail the effects global warming has in relation to various climate changes—rising temperatures, an increase or decrease in rainfall, etc.—and how these affect other aspects of life.
- Discuss in more detail the causes of and solutions to the problem of global warming.
- Nitrogen oxide is a by-product of burning fuel.
- Nitrous oxide is a by-product of burning fuel.
- Quiz questions relating to this section may be found on page 13.

Answers

page 46

1. (a) average   (b) temperature   (c) humans   (d) greenhouse   (e) major   (f) trap
   (g) space   (h) carbon dioxide   (i) methane   (j) fossil   (k) industry   (l) oxygen
   (m) climate   (n) rate   (o) area   (p) sea   (q) all   (r) respiratory
   (s) heat   (t) 6°F (2.3°C)   (u) reduce   (v) sources   (w) trees   (x) environment

page 47

Teacher check

Cross-Curricular Activities

- Students investigate average yearly temperatures and rainfall figures for their region over the past 20 years and draw conclusions relating to global warming.
- Students draw diagrams or flow charts which show how a change in one aspect of climate may affect plants and animals.
- Students use dark paints or other media to create representations of how the Earth could look if global warming is fact and increases.

What is global warming?

Global warming is the general term used to describe an average increase in the temperature of the Earth.

How is global warming caused?

> Global warming may be a direct result of human activities.
>
> The greenhouse effect is one aspect of global warming.

The temperature of the Earth can rise as a result of an increase in the amount of greenhouse gases in the atmosphere. Gases such as carbon dioxide, nitrous oxide and methane trap energy from the sun, preventing the heat from going back out into space and letting the Earth cool. This is the same effect created in a greenhouse, where glass panels are used to trap the sun's warmth to grow plants.

Burning fossil fuels (coal, oil and gas) for industrial and domestic use releases the majority of gases into the atmosphere. Homes and industry are powered by electricity, which is mainly produced by burning fossil fuels in power plants. Cars and trucks use fossil fuels to provide energy. Animals, such as dairy cattle, and rubbish in landfills produce a gas called methane. As the population of the world increases, so do greenhouse gases.

Trees convert carbon dioxide to oxygen and release it into the atmosphere. As more trees are cut down (deforestation), it becomes more difficult to cope with the greenhouse gases, which further adds to global warming. Trees also regulate and cool the world's climate. As more trees are cut down, climate changes become more unpredictable.

What effects does global warming have?

Global warming causes climate change. Climate is the pattern of weather conditions occurring in a given place over a long period of time. Climate change is a naturally-occurring event, but it is the rapid rate of change created by humans that is causing concern among many scientists. Changes to climate may have many effects, including an increase or decrease in rainfall, temperatures in

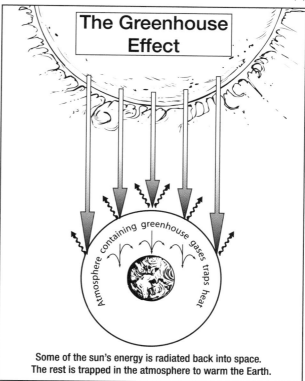

The Greenhouse Effect

Atmosphere containing greenhouse gases traps heat

Some of the sun's energy is radiated back into space. The rest is trapped in the atmosphere to warm the Earth.

an area becoming warmer or colder, rising sea levels, altering delicate ecosystems, and affecting the ability to predict weather patterns for farming. Changes to climate will affect all plants and animals on Earth!

Not only do greenhouse gases contribute to climate change, they also cause health problems, such as an increase in skin cancers, respiratory problems due to poor air quality, heat stress, and a possible increase in diseases such as malaria.

How can the problem of global warming be solved?

The Earth has warmed by 1°F (0.38°C) in the last 100 years. Scientists expect an increase in average global temperatures of between 2°F (0.76°C) and 6°F (2.3°C) in the next 100 years. The most important way to alleviate global warming is by reducing the amount of greenhouse gases being produced. This can be done by reusing and recycling resources, using alternative power sources, planting trees, and encouraging people to take care of the environment.

Fact File

The temperature at the middle of the last ice age, about 18,000 years ago, was only 7°F (2.7°C) cooler than it is today!

Use the text on page 45 to complete the cloze.

1. Global warming is the general term used to describe an _____ [a]
   increase in the _____ [b] of the Earth. It is caused by the activities of
   _____ [c] The more people there are, the more _____ [d]
   gases are produced.

   Greenhouse gases are a _____ [e] contributor to the problem of global
   warming. Greenhouse gases _____ [f] the heat from the sun preventing it
   from going back into _____ [g] and cooling the Earth.

   Some greenhouse gases include _____ [h], nitrogen oxide and
   _____ [i]. Most greenhouse gases are produced by _____ [j]
   fuels used in homes and _____ [k] and in transportation vehicles. Methane
   gas created in landfills also adds to greenhouse gases.

   Chopping down trees leaves the greenhouse gas carbon dioxide in the air, because
   carbon dioxide is not being converted to _____ [l]. Global warming causes
   _____ [m] change. Even though climate changes occur naturally, many
   scientists are concerned about the _____ [n] of change. Climate change
   affects rainfall, temperatures in a specific _____ [o], _____ [p]
   levels, delicate ecosystems, and farming. In fact, _____ [q] plants and
   animals on Earth will be affected! The health problems for humans due to global warming
   may include an increase in skin cancers, _____ [r] problems due to poor
   air quality, _____ [s] stress and a possible increase in diseases such as
   malaria.

   Scientists expect global temperatures to increase by as much as _____ [t]
   in the next one hundred years. The solution to alleviating global warming is to
   _____ [u] the amount of greenhouse gases by recycling and reusing
   resources, finding other _____ [v] of power, planting _____ [w]
   and encouraging people to take care of the _____ [x].

Every Little Bit Helps!

1. Complete the table below by giving one solution for each of the problems contributing to greenhouse gases which cause global warming. Write solutions which you can implement in your home, local community or nationally.

Problem	Solution		
	Home	Local	National
Mom drives you to school and sports practice every day.			
Your fridge is a big one which is constantly being used.			
The backyard is large and bare, consisting mainly of grass.			
The trash can is always very heavy and full on trash days.			
Mom loves her garden and won't let your friends and you go near her plants.			
All your kitchen appliances are powered by electricity.			

Using alternative sources of power is one way to reduce greenhouse gases and alleviate global warming.

2. For each application, give an alternative, workable power source.

   (a) cooking _____   (b) warmth _____

   (c) transportation _____   (d) cooling _____

3. On a separate sheet of paper, design a car for the not-too-distant future which employs an alternative source of fuel. You may use Internet research to help you.

Fact File

Scientists gather information about the temperature of the Earth using weather stations, weather balloons, ocean buoys, weather satellites, ice core samples, soil and rock analysis, and even tree rings!

Ozone Depletion

Indicators

- *Reads information and answers questions about ozone depletion.*
- *Completes a design for a poster encouraging CFC awareness.*

Worksheet Information

- All "hot" objects in space, including stars, give off ultraviolet (UV) radiation. Ultraviolet rays are those which lie outside the visible spectrum at the violet end. UV rays are those responsible for causing sunburn. Although most UV waves are blocked from entering the Earth's atmosphere by gases such as ozone, on some days more UV waves will get through. For this reason, scientists have developed a UV index to keep people informed about harmful UV waves so that they can protect themselves accordingly.

- Ultraviolet light has shorter wavelengths than visible light. UV light is invisible to humans but visible to some insects such as bees. Scientists have divided the UV part of the spectrum into three regions (near, far and extreme ultraviolet) which are distinguished by how energetic the radiation is and by the wavelength of the light.

- Discuss the types of drawings students will need to complete in order to complete page 50. Students may draw creative sketches to show their understanding of what an ozone molecule is. Labels should be included. Diagrams would be more appropriate for answering Questions 2 and 3, while a selection of small pictures such as a refrigerator, a cleaning product, or a fire extinguisher will suffice for Question 4. Drawings for Question 5 may be more imaginative and may include alternate ways to keep food fresh or to keep the house cool in summer, "inspectors" to record and fine households emitting too many CFCs, etc.
  Note: CFCs are no longer used as propellants in aerosol cans in most countries.

- Quiz questions relating to this section may be found on page 13.

Answers

page 50

    1–5. Teacher check

page 51

    Teacher check

Cross-Curricular Activities

- Students write an imaginative text from the point of view of the Earth having its ozone layer destroyed by CFCs .

- Students write an acrostic poem about ozone.

- Students investigate, tally and graph a list of CFCs used at home.

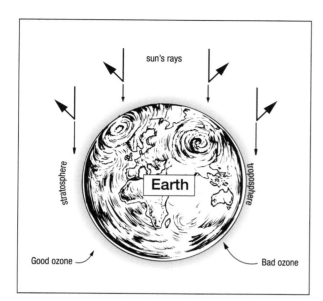

sun's rays

stratosphere

troposphere

Earth

Good ozone —

Bad ozone

What is ozone?

Ozone is a molecule consisting of three oxygen atoms joined together (O_3). It is colorless and has a very harsh odor. It is less common than normal oxygen.

The effects of ozone vary greatly depending on its location. About 90 percent of all ozone is produced naturally in the upper atmosphere or stratosphere, where it performs a very important task.

The ozone in the lower few miles, close to the surface of the Earth (the troposphere), reacts with sunlight, organic compounds and nitrogen oxides to form pollutants which are harmful to living things. Ozone at ground level forms a major component of smog. Most ozone forms over the Equator, where the greatest amount of sunlight hits the Earth. Winds then carry it to higher altitudes. The amount of ozone in the stratosphere will vary from place to place, depending on latitude, seasons and daily weather conditions.

What is the ozone layer?

Ozone which builds up in the upper atmosphere filters out harmful ultraviolet radiation from the sun and protects all living things on Earth. The ozone layer is not really a layer at all. It is simply called this because

the ozone particles are scattered within the upper layer of the atmosphere. Without the ozone layer to provide protection, harmful ultraviolet rays would cause health problems for people, including skin cancers, eye cataracts and a reduced immunity to disease. It would also damage microscopic life in the ocean which forms the basis of the marine food chain. A loss of ozone in the stratosphere even affects the climate of the world.

What is the ozone hole?

Ozone can be depleted. When this happens, ozone thins out and is less effective at deflecting ultraviolet rays from the sun. This depletion or "thinning out" is commonly called the "ozone hole." Ozone thinning occurs every spring above the Antarctic and, to a lesser degree, above the Arctic, where weather conditions and very low air temperatures speed up and enhance ozone loss by manufactured chemicals.

What causes the ozone layer to deplete?

In an atmosphere free of pollution, there is a natural balance between the amount of ozone being produced and the amount being destroyed, so the amount of ozone remains fairly constant. When chlorofluorocarbons (CFCs) are released into the atmosphere, ozone is destroyed, allowing more harmful ultraviolet rays to reach the Earth's surface. Manufactured CFCs are the major cause of ozone depletion in the stratosphere. CFCs can be found in coolants in refrigeration and air conditioners, as solvents in cleaning products, in electronic circuit boards, in fire extinguishers, and as propellants in aerosols (in some countries).

Can ozone depletion be fixed?

An international treaty called the Montreal Protocol was signed in 1987. The participating nations agreed to reduce the use of CFCs and other ozone depleting substances by half by 2000. Amendments in 1990 and 1992 changed the deadline to January 1 2005, with full elimination of CFC use by 2010. Some experts believe that global ozone levels should recover some time in the next century.

Ozone Depletion - 2

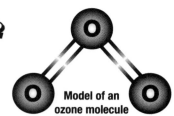

Model of an ozone molecule

Use the text on page 49 and diagrams or drawings to show your understanding of the following:

1. An oxygen molecule:	2. The two different types of ozone — both good and harmful:
3. The ozone hole over the Antarctic:	4. The causes of ozone depletion:

5. Some suggestions for combating ozone depletion:

Fact File

CFCs have a life span in the atmosphere of between 20 to 100 years or more, so one chlorine atom can destroy ozone molecules for a very long time!

ENVIRONMENTAL ISSUES

"CFC Awareness" Poster

Complete the information for a poster designed to make people aware of the harmful effects of using CFC products.

1. Write the words or phrases you will include to explain what CFCs are and what they do. (You may use bullet points.)

2. List any drawings or diagrams you may need to include to help your explanation of what CFCs do.

3. Select and write some appropriate colors for your headings, background or borders which will highlight the importance of CFC reduction.

4. Write some "catchy" phrases which may be used as a title or headings.

5. Complete a detailed drawing of what your finished poster design will look like.

6. Use large sheet of paper to create your poster, then display it in a prominent area of the school.

7. Evaluate your completed design by coloring the stars.

☆ ☆ ☆ ☆ ☆
DREADFUL   AWESOME

Fact File

Ozone is measured in Dobson Units (DU). Normal ozone concentration is about 300 to 350 DU. An "ozone hole" exists when ozone levels fall below 200 DU.

Soil Degradation

Indicators

- *Reads information and answers questions about soil degradation.*
- *Completes an interview with a gardener about his/her gardening techniques.*

Worksheet Information

- Some experts claim that erosion is the main cause of soil degradation globally, with water erosion being most harmful. Soils are normally protected from erosion by plant stems and leaves above ground, which act as a barrier to wind and water. Underground, the soil is anchored by the roots of the plants. Farming increases the risk of erosion because it disturbs the vegetation when the land is prepared, tilled or overgrazed. In some countries, particularly Canada and the U.S., farmers are using a technique called "conservation tillage" or "zero tillage," which employs special machinery and herbicides to plant crops with minimal disturbance to the soil.

- Students may complete the interview questionnaire from memory if they have a good knowledge of (or actually help) a parent or grandparent in the garden.

- Quiz questions relating to this section may be found on page 14.

Answers

page 54

1. Soil degradation is the name used when damage is done to the land which reduces its ability to produce quality agricultural products.

2. excessive use of pesticides and fertilizers, soil compaction by heavy equipment during building works or farming, erosion by water and wind, waterlogging, increased salination, overgrazing

3. toxic to certain crops; contaminate agricultural workers, animals and streams

4. Heavy machines compact the soil, making water drain away rather than down into the roots of the plants where it is needed, and reducing the spaces for oxygen around the roots of the plants so they can't "breathe."

5. Soil erosion occurs when wind or water moves soil from one place to another.

6. Salination occurs when the water table rises, bringing salt to the surface and making the soil unfit for many plants.

7. Overgrazing can destroy good topsoil and remove vegetation, making the land more easily eroded.

8. Answers may include four of the following: planting trees, safer crop production, better use of heavy equipment, windbreaks, careful irrigation practices, slope terracing, using saline-resistant plants and improving soils by adding organic matter.

page 55

Teacher check

Cross-Curricular Activities

- Students draw diagrams which show how plants protect the soil from being eroded or flow charts which show how soil degradation can affect the economy of a country.

- Students gain permission to select and take care of a section of the school garden, improving the soil with organic matter, selecting appropriate plants, planting them and caring for them.

- Students study gardening maps with colored soil zones to investigate the type(s) of soil in their area.

Most people are aware of the effects of water and air pollution on the environment. The importance of soil, however, is often overlooked. As the population of the world continues to grow, the need for food and fiber products increases, as does the need for more homes and roads. Degradation of the soil is a worldwide environmental problem.

What is soil degradation?

Soil degradation is the name used when any damage is done to the land which reduces its ability to produce quality agricultural products.

What causes soil degradation?

Soil degradation has a number of causes usually resulting from poor agricultural practices. Some reasons include:

- excessive use of pesticides and fertilizers,
- soil compaction by heavy equipment during building works or farming,
- erosion by wind or water,
- waterlogging,
- increased salinity,
- overgrazing by cattle and sheep.

The long-term use of pesticides and fertilizers can leave chemicals in the soil which can have toxic effects on certain crops and can contaminate agricultural workers, livestock and nearby streams.

Compacted soils have poor drainage, have reduced spaces for oxygen around the roots of plants, and have hard surfaces which encourage water to run off instead of down into the soil where it is needed.

Soil erosion occurs when wind or water move soil from one place to another. Soils erode quickly when there is no vegetation to hold the soil in place. The rate of soil erosion is increasing rapidly as a result of human activities.

Waterlogged soils occur as groundwater close to the soil surface rises, making land unproductive.

Salination occurs when the water table rises and salt is forced to the surface. Often this is due to the removal of trees. High levels of salt make soil unsuitable for plant growth.

Overgrazing of sheep and cattle has the effect of destroying quality topsoil and removing vegetation, which makes the land more susceptible to erosion by wind and water.

Why is it important not to degrade soil?

People depend on the land to supply food, materials for clothing, ingredients for medicines, and wood for building and heating. Good quality soil is needed to supply the essentials to sustain human life.

What can be done to retain the quality of soil?

Better land management practices are vital to prevent soil degradation. Activities such as planting trees to reclaim land, safer crop production, better use of heavy equipment, the use of windbreaks, careful irrigation practices, terracing of slopes, using saline-resistant plants, and improving soils by adding organic matter are some possible ways to combat this problem.

Use the text on page 53 to answer the questions.

1. What is soil degradation?

_____

_____

_____

_____

2. Name six causes of soil degradation.

- _____

  _____

- _____

  _____

- _____

  _____

- _____

  _____

- _____

  _____

- _____

  _____

3. What detrimental effect can the long-term use of pesticides and fertilizers have on soils?

_____

_____

_____

_____

4. Why is it necessary to be careful when using heavy machines for farming and building?

_____

_____

_____

5. How does soil erosion occur?

_____

_____

_____

_____

6. How does salination of the soil occur?

_____

_____

_____

_____

7. What effect can sheep and cattle have on soils?

_____

_____

_____

8. Name four ways to combat soil degradation.

_____

_____

_____

_____

Fact File

Adding clay to sandy soils improves their ability to hold water; adding sand to clay soils improves their ability to drain excess water away.

Gardener Interview

1. Select an adult who enjoys gardening to interview. Ask him/her the following questions and write his/her answers.

Name of Gardener:	
Location:	
(a) What type of plants do you like to grow?	
(b) What kind of soil do you have? (sandy, clay, etc.)	
(c) What kinds of fertilizers and pesticides do you use and what are they for?	
(d) What have you done to try to improve the soil?	
(e) Are there any other things you do which help when growing your plants? (For example, rotating crops, "companion planting," dig in old crops to improve the soil, etc.)	

2. Is this person a good gardener? Yes No

3. Is he/she helping to combat soil degradation in his/her area? Yes No

4. If "Yes," describe how? If "No," suggest how he/she could improve his/her method of gardening.

Fact File

Soils can be measured to see how acidic they are. They are given a "ph" value on a scale between 0 and 14 (7 is neutral!). Very acidic soils are unsuitable for many crops.

- *Reads information and answers questions about genetically-modified foods.*
- *Prepares for a debate by planning arguments for and against GM foods.*

Worksheet Information

- Genes from the DNA of one species can be transferred to the DNA of another species; from plant to plant, animal to animal, animal to plant or plant to animal. Besides the environmental advantages and disadvantages outlined on page 57, there are also health, social, cultural and economic advantages and disadvantages to consider. More research needs to done in this area before concerns and benefits are fully understood.
- Quiz questions relating to this section can be found on page 14.

Answers

page 58

1. A gene is one of the tiny units that pass on the characteristics of a living thing.
2. Teacher check
3. Teacher check
4. (a) less, pesticides
   (b) poultry, immunity
   (c) increased, lower
   (d) salinity
   (e) poison

5. Possible answers could include:
   (a) What could happen if pollen from a GM crop was blown in the wind and other plants were fertilized?
   (b) What could happen if GM crops outgrew the native flora in an area?
6. Many species of plants and animals are linked in a food chain, and the introduction of a plant, for example, that produces a poison that kills a pest might also be harmful to other species in the food chain.

page 59

Teacher check

Cross-Curricular Activities

- Research to find other reasons foods have been modified or people are attempting to modify them besides those discussed on page 57. Examples are bananas that will produce vaccines against diseases such as Hepatitis B, and coffee bushes where the coffee beans ripen at the same time rather than a few at a time, saving labor costs and controlling the time of harvesting.
- Look at the labeling of foods in the supermarket to see if any have been genetically modified.
- Look at Web sites on the Internet that give information for and against GM foods.

Genetically-modified (GM) food has to do with "genes." A gene is one of the tiny units that pass on the characteristics of a living thing;  e.g., it gives a carrot an orange color or a human the same kind of hair as his or her mother or father. If a food product has been genetically modified, it means it has had a gene taken from a living thing and placed into it. Scientists who do this work are called genetic engineers. They found that they could change or modify the characteristics of a food crop by using genes from other sources.

Why are GM foods made?

 They are made for reasons such as creating crops that are resistant to insects or disease without having to use harmful pesticides, making food stay fresher longer, or producing a larger crop.

What are some examples of GM foods?

Rice crops in poorer parts of Asia are now rich in vitamin A to help prevent early blindness among the population, whose diet is mainly just rice. Some crops carry a poison that kills pests. Salmon are being farmed that grow three times faster than a wild salmon, helping reduce overfishing problems while being cheaper to produce.

What are some environmental advantages of GM foods?

- GM foods may help the environment by using less water, fertilizer and pesticide.

- As GM crops generally have larger yields, this means increased production and lower food costs, a factor in attacking the problem of world hunger.

- GM foods containing vaccines for poultry and livestock could boost immunity against diseases in these animals.

- GM crops can be grown in areas suffering from salinity and drought.

What problems could GM foods cause to the environment?

- Other crops can be fertilized by pollen from GM crops being blown in the wind, resulting in uncontrolled changes taking place to another crop that hasn't been tested to carry that gene.

- Unknown viruses could result from the mass production of GM crops.

- Pests may develop resistance to the crops that have been created to kill them.

- There is concern that GM crops might outgrow the native flora in an area and lessen the amount and range of native plants. This could also lead to a reduced food supply for birds and other wildlife.

- GM crops could cause ecological side effects. Many species of plants and animals are linked in a food chain and the introduction of a plant, for example, that produces a poison that kills a pest might also be harmful to other species in the food chain.

The debate for and against GM foods will continue for some time, until further studies can show for sure whether or not they present serious threats to the environment or are a gift to humanity.

Use the text on page 57 to answer the questions.

1. Write a definition for the word "gene." _____

_____

2. Give an example from the text or one of your own to explain something a gene can pass on.

3. Give an example of a GM food and the reason it was developed.

_____

_____

4. Complete the sentences to explain some environmental advantages of GM foods.

   (a) GM foods use _____ water, fertilizer and _____.

   (b) Vaccines for _____ and livestock could boost _____ against diseases.

   (c) GM crops generally have larger yields, which means _____ production and _____ food costs.

   (d) GM crops can be grown in areas suffering from _____ and drought.

   (e) Some GM crops carry a _____ that kills pests.

5. Write a question for these answers.

   (a) Uncontrolled changes could take place in another crop that hasn't been tested to carry that gene. _____

   _____

   (b) It could lessen the amount and range of native plants.

   _____

6. Explain how GM crops could upset the balance of a food chain.

_____

_____

_____

Fact File

A GM plant has been grown containing a gene from a luminescent jellyfish. It is planted alongside a crop and glows in the dark when it experiences a lack of water! The farmer then knows to water the crop.

GM Foods – For or Against?

Genetically-Modified Foods

GM food technology promises many benefits, but there are also concerns it may cause problems in the environment.

1. With a partner, plan arguments for and against GM food production, using the information on page 57 and other facts you have found out in class discussions or researched on the Internet or in the library.

Arguments For:

Arguments Against:

2. Now form groups of nine and allocate responsibilities for the debate. Fill in the names below. Prepare and practice the debate in separate teams, combining notes, before holding the actual debate.

Chairperson	Timekeeper	Adjudicator
Affirmative Speaker 1	Affirmative Speaker 2	Affirmative Speaker 3
Negative Speaker 1	Negative Speaker 2	Negative Speaker 3

> **Fact File**
>
> *The first commercial GM food was a slow-ripening tomato. It was kept on the vine longer before picking so it would taste better, but not rot quickly on the store shelf like other tomatoes would. However, they didn't ship well as they were softer and production stopped.*

Urbanization

Indicators

- *Reads information and answers questions about the effects urbanization can have on the environment.*
- *Compares the environmental problems faced by a developing and a developed city and how these problems could be solved.*

Worksheet Information

- Some positive effects of urbanization could be discussed with the students, not just the environmental problems outlined on page 61. Two examples include:
  - It is more efficient to supply energy, water, heating and waste disposal to people concentrated in houses and medium or high density accommodation than to those separated by acres of land.
  - Access to health, education, social services, cultural events, recreational activities etc. is more convenient in cities, especially if the public transportation system is efficient.

  Students could add further benefits after discussions.

- Quiz questions relating to this section can be found on page 15.

Answers

page 62

1. Urbanization is the increase in the proportion of people living in towns and cities.
2. people moving from the country to the city, birth rate, new industry being developed
3. Teacher check
4. They are potentially more difficult in developing countries as regulations are more difficult to enforce.
5. Native animals and plants can be relocated.

page 63

Teacher check

Cross-Curricular Activities

- Students can discuss problems other than environmental that occur due to urbanization; e.g., the social problems of slum areas and poor living conditions, or unemployment and crime.
- Order urban areas according to their population in student's own state, country, etc. Identify any environmental problems in each location.
- Debate "It is better to live in the city than the country."

Urbanization

Urbanization is the increase in the proportion of people living in towns and cities. It occurs when people move from rural (country) areas to urban (city and town) areas or the population of an area increases to urban proportions through birth rate, a new industry being developed, etc. A densely populated urban center may have hundreds of thousands or even millions of people, while other urban centers may only have a few thousand.

Urbanization can have a significant impact on the surrounding environment. The major environmental issues include habitat destruction, water pollution, and air and noise pollution from urban traffic.

Habitat Destruction

In the process of urbanization, land is needed to create and further develop urban centers. Native habitats makes way for residential areas, roads, industries and recreational areas to support the population, which means that animal and plant habitats are destroyed.

Water Pollution

When an area is urbanized, water that falls as rain is channelled into run-off systems instead of being absorbed into the soil. It picks up ground pollutants, which could be in the form of industrial waste products, insufficiently treated sewage, or even litter. If an area is in a coastal region, the surrounding seas could become polluted with waste discharges from industry or sewage systems. The problems are potentially worse in high density urban areas and in cities of the developing world, where regulations are difficult to enforce.

One way of disposing of urban waste is by depositing it in landfill sites. Problems can occur if these sites are poorly managed and waste contaminates soil and groundwater. Groundwater becomes more depleted (decreases) as it becomes more polluted. Water pollution is a concern to public health and also affects animals and plants.

Air and Noise Pollution

Air pollution, particularly in larger urban areas, is a serious problem, as there are so many cars and factories. Motor vehicle exhausts, gases and chemicals from emissions by industries, and smoke from wood heaters are among the main ways the air becomes polluted. Large blankets of smog often cover large cities. Air pollution is a public health problem and also contributes to the thinning of the ozone layer, which is like a sunscreen for the Earth.

Overcrowded environments lead to the problem of noise pollution. Traffic noise can be annoying and disturbing. A quieter environment creates a more relaxed and healthier community.

In summary, the denser the urban population the more problems for the environment. Urban environments in developed and developing countries experience similar problems. Nations with a stronger economy generally have stricter guidelines in place about pollution, the monitoring of habitat destruction and the relocation of native animals and plants.

Urbanization - 2

Use the text on page 61 to answer the questions.

1. Write a definition for the term "urbanization." _____
   _____

2. List three ways urbanization can occur.

   • _____

   • _____

   • _____

3. Write key words and phrases under each heading to explain how urbanization can affect the environment.

Habitat Destruction	*Water Pollution*
Air Pollution	*Noise Pollution*

4. Why are the problems associated with urbanization potentially more difficult to overcome in developing countries?

   _____

   _____

5. Name one way the effects of habitat destruction could be overcome.

   _____

   _____

Fact File

Densely populated urban areas can be up to 50°F warmer than their surrounding rural areas. This is a result of factors such as the concentration of heat sources and the reflection of heat on huge paved areas, as compared to the absorption of heat by vegetation.

Comparing Urban Problems

How similar or different are the environmental problems faced by developing and industrialized urban areas? What is being done or needs to be done to solve these problems?

1. Your task is to choose a densely populated developing city and a developed city; e.g., Dhaka (Bangladesh), population 9,300,000 and Tokyo (Japan), population 36,500,000. Research to find two major environmental concerns for each that are caused by urbanization, what has been or is being done to ease each problem, and what could be done if nothing has been done so far.

CITY:	Developing/Developed
Problem 1:	
Solving the Problem	
Problem 2:	
Solving the Problem	

CITY:	Developing/Developed
Problem 1:	
Solving the Problem	
Problem 2:	
Solving the Problem	

> **Fact file**
>
> *It is thought that in the next 50 years, two-thirds of the world's population will be living in cities and towns.*

Natural Disasters

Indicators

- *Reads information and answers questions about natural disasters and their effect on the environment.*
- *Researches to find information about the environmental effects of four natural disasters.*

Worksheet Information

- In researching the activity on page 67, students could type in the name, date and place of the disasters listed into a search engine on the Internet. Alternatively, they could find other disasters by typing in key words such as "natural disasters," "volcanic eruptions," etc.
- Quiz questions relating to this section can be found on page 15.

Answers

page 66

1. Teacher check
2. (a) forms over the Indian or southern Pacific Ocean
   (b) forms over the Atlantic Ocean
   (c) forms over the western Pacific Ocean
3. (a) volcanoes (purple)
   (b) tornadoes (orange)
   (c) drought (gray)
   (d) tsunamis (blue)
   (e) wildfires (red)
   (f) cyclones, hurricanes, typhoons (green)
   (g) avalanches, landslides, mudslides (yellow)
   (h) floods (white)
   (i) earthquakes (brown)

4. (a) False
   (b) True
   (c) True
   (d) False
   (e) False
   (f) True

page 67

Teacher check

Cross-Curricular Activities

- Construct a time line on a bulletin board illustrating a selection of different types of natural disasters and the destruction they caused to people and the environment.
- Research to find out the emergency procedures to follow if students are caught in a wildfire, a cyclone is approaching their town, floodwaters are rising, etc.
- Follow the continuing clean-up process and the recovery of the environment for the recent natural disasters of the Boxing Day tsunami, 2004, and Hurricane Katrina, New Orleans, 2005.

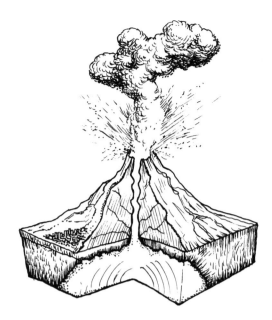

A disaster is a sudden event that causes great damage and harm to living and nonliving things and can have long-lasting or even permanent effects on the environment. It can be caused by humans; e.g., a massive oil spill—or be created by a force of nature; e.g., a volcanic eruption. Examples of some possible natural disasters are outlined below.

Tsunamis

"Tsunami" is a Japanese word meaning "a long, low wave," as seen in a harbor. They are caused by volcanic eruptions, coastal earthquakes, or undersea landslides. Tsunamis can cause great damage when the monstrous waves, as high as 300 feet, explode on the shore and continue over the land, sweeping up everything in their path and causing widespread flooding.

Earthquakes

Earthquakes are the shaking of the ground caused by rock shifting along a "fault," or break, in the Earth's crust, where the plates of rock meet. People (and animals) can be injured or killed as structures collapse. Earthquakes can cause landslides, avalanches and tsunamis, resulting in other ways for people, wildlife and the environment to be harmed.

Drought

Drought is the lack of rainfall over a long period of time. It affects more people (and the environment) than any other disaster. Effects include loss of stock (and feed), dust storms, wildfires, famine, soil erosion and vegetation loss.

Flood

Floods are the most common natural disaster and occur when a body of water rises and overflows onto normally dry land. They are destructive to people, property and the environment. Water can become contaminated with sewage, garbage, and animal and human corpses.

Volcanoes

A volcano is a place on the Earth's surface through which melted rock (known as "magma") and gas erupt. Volcanic eruptions can cause great devastation as they spill hot lava, ash, dust, gas and cinders over large areas, killing and burying people, animals, and plants and destroying buildings.

Cyclones, Hurricanes and Typhoons

These are areas of extreme low pressure which are characterized by rotating winds around a calm, central "eye." They are called cyclones if they form over the Indian or southern Pacific Ocean, hurricanes if they form over the Atlantic Ocean and typhoons if they form over the western Pacific Ocean. They often produce destructive winds and large amounts of rain, which cause structural damage and flooding, harming people and the environment.

Tornadoes

Tornadoes are violent whirling winds. They move over the Earth like a giant vacuum cleaner, destroying everything in their path.

Wildfires

Wildfires are one of the most destructive forces in nature. They become disasters when heavy smoke and showers of embers are fanned by strong winds, causing loss of life and injury to humans and stock and damage to property and vegetation. Trees can generally regenerate and plant growth can be improved, but animals cannot always escape from a fire.

Avalanches, Landslides and Mudslides

Avalanches, landslides and mudslides can occur from various triggers such as an earthquake, change in temperature, heavy rain or volcanic eruption, resulting in widespread deaths, injuries and damage to the environment.

Natural Disasters - 2

Use the text on page 65 to answer the questions.

Use the text on page 65 to answer the questions.

Fact File

The word "disaster" comes from the Italian word "disastrato," meaning "not having a lucky star."

1. Give an example of a …

    (a) human-created disaster. _____

    (b) natural disaster. _____

2. Explain where each of these storms forms.

    (a) cyclone _____

    (b) hurricane _____

    (c) typhoon _____

3. Read the quick facts below about natural disasters. Shade or highlight each box according to the code.

tsunami .... *(blue)*	volcano .... *(purple)*	earthquake .... *(brown)*
flood .... *(white)*	drought ....*(gray)*	wildfire .... *(red)*
tornado.....*(orange)*	avalanche, mudslide, landslide .... *(yellow)*	
cyclone, hurricane, typhoon...................... *(green)*		

(a) devastation caused by hot lava, ash, dust, gas and cinders	(b) destroys everything like a giant vacuum cleaner	(c) effects include loss of stock, dust storms, wildfires, soil erosion and vegetation loss
(d) monstrous waves explode on the shore, sweeping up everything in their path	(e) become disasters when they cause loss of human life, stock and wildlife	(f) produce destructive winds and large amounts of rain, harming people and the environment
(g) occur from various triggers such as an earthquake, change in temperature, heavy rain or volcanic eruption	(h) water can become contaminated from sewage, garbage and animal and human corpses	(i) can cause landslides, avalanches and tsunamis

4. Answer True or False.

    (a) The eye of a cyclone is violent .... True] False

    (b) Earthquakes occur along fault lines .... True] False

    (c) A tsunami can be as high as 300 feet .... True] False

    (d) Wildfires are the most common natural disaster. .... True] False

    (e) A hurricane forms over the Pacific Ocean..................................... True] False

    (f) Tornadoes are a type of wind... True] False

Natural Disasters Retrieval Chart

There have been so many natural disasters in recorded history that it would take pages to describe them all! Your task, with a partner, is to research four natural disasters and use key words and phrases to complete the information under each heading. You can choose from the list below or use others you find in your research.

- *Great Fire of London* *1666*
- *Great drowning in Holland* *1362*
- *Eruption of Mt. Vesuvius, Italy* .... *79 A.D.*
- *Boxing Day tsunami, Indian Ocean* *2004*
- *Hurricane Katrina, New Orleans* *2005*
- *Earthquake, Lisbon, Portugal* *1755*
- *Indian drought* *1900*
- *Landslide, Peru* *1970*
- *Tornado, Bangladesh* *1989*

Type of Disaster	When and Where It Happened	What Happened/Loss of Life/Damage	Environmental Effects

Fact File

A tornado is the most unpredictable and violent storm. It may travel slowly or as fast as 60 mph. A tornado may move along the ground a few yards or travel a few hundred miles. It might skip along or even suddenly make a U-turn!

Indicators

- *Reads information and answers questions about reducing, reusing and recycling.*
- *Completes an experiment about garbage decomposing.*

Worksheet Information

- Students should be familiar with the "three Rs," but may not be as familiar with the relationship between garbage, greenhouse gases and global warming.
- Quiz questions relating to this section may be found on page 16.

Answers

page 70

1. (b)
2. (a), (d), (e)
3. Teacher check

page 71

Teacher check

Cross-Curricular Activities

- Students begin a "garbage reduction chart" for use at home over a week to see how many small steps they can make which may reduce the amount of garbage entering the environment.
- Students design and create holders for their desks at school using recycled materials.
- Students investigate community facilities for recycling materials, such as clothing bins or centers for recycling green waste, and find ways to use them.

The population of the world continues to grow, people are living longer and the desire to own material possessions continues. Unfortunately, the process of producing and consuming goods produces waste.

Waste is anything discarded and released into the environment which may have an impact on it. More and more waste is being created and landfill areas (areas for disposing of garbage) fill up very quickly.

Garbage decomposing in landfill areas is an environmental problem, as it produces two greenhouse gases: carbon dioxide and methane, an invisible, odorless and highly flammable gas. Methane contributes to the problem of global warming as it accumulates in the atmosphere. Some landfill sites are able to collect methane and burn it to produce energy. Waste buried in landfills can also pollute underground water if not managed properly.

Garbage can only break down when water and oxygen are present — both of which are very valuable resources. Consequently, garbage buried in landfills often decomposes very slowly.

Some solid wastes can be incinerated under strict controls. Unfortunately, burning rubbish can produce unhealthy gases, carbon dioxide or toxic chemicals which must be treated so that acid rain, ozone depletion and air pollution are not the result. The ashes must be disposed of carefully at a landfill or hazardous waste facility if they are toxic.

Recycling offers one way to reduce the impact that waste disposal has on the environment. Reducing the amount of waste produced and reusing nonrenewable products are other ways.

Recycling, including composting, turns a waste product into the same product or something different so that it can be used again as a valuable resource. Glass, metal, paper, aluminum and plastics can be collected, separated and reprocessed into new materials or products. Some other items which can be recycled include acid batteries, building materials, chemicals, electronic equipment, lead, oil, paint, tires, white goods (household appliances such as refrigerators) and garden waste. Recycling conserves resources for the future, prevents the emission of greenhouse gases and water pollutants, saves energy, supplies raw materials to industry, creates jobs, reduces the need for new landfills and incinerators and encourages the development of "greener" technologies.

Reducing the amount of waste produced means making more careful choices each day. Some ways this can be done include purchasing items which last longer, selecting products which have little or no packaging (especially nontoxic packaging), using natural resources wisely, refusing plastic bags given out by stores, refusing "junk" mail, starting a garden, or composting kitchen scraps.

Reusing simply means to use the same item many times instead of disposing of it after one use. Reusing saves the energy and resources which are used to make a new product and means the product doesn't become more garbage. Reusing may be as simple as donating something to a charity or community group, repairing it, or selling it. Reusing means that something does not have to be reprocessed, so it is better than recycling. Some simple ways to reuse include using durable mugs and napkins, refilling bottles, reusing boxes, using empty jars for leftover food, buying refillable pencils, holding a garage sale to dispose of unwanted goods, reusing plastic plates and cutlery, or repairing an old bicycle.

Use the text on page 69 to answer the questions.

1. Select the correct statement from those given and write it on the line.

    (a) Waste is anything which is discarded.

    (b) Waste is anything discarded and released into the environment which may have an impact on it.

    (c) Waste is an area on the body.

    _____

    _____

2. Underline the correct statements.

    (a) Decomposing garbage produces two greenhouse gases: carbon dioxide and methane.

    (b) Methane contributes to global warming because it accumulates in the atmosphere and has no worthwhile use.

    (c) Some solid wastes can be burned, which relieves one environmental problem.

    (d) In order to decompose, garbage needs water and oxygen.

    (e) Ashes from burned solid waste must be disposed of carefully as some may be toxic.

3. Complete the table for the "three Rs."

	Recycling	**Reducing**	**Reusing**
What is it?			
How can it be done?			
What advantages does it have?			

Fact File

"Closed loop recycling" is the name used to describe an old product being made into the same thing again. For example, old aluminum cans become new aluminum cans; old glass jars become new glass jars, and so on!

Landfill Experiment

1. Follow the procedure to find which materials will decompose and which will not. Check each part of the experiment as you complete it.

(a) *Collect your materials:*

- [ ] large glass or plastic jar
- [ ] various pieces of garbage; e.g., food scraps, bones, metal, paper, plastic
- [ ] garden soil (NOT potting mix) and water
- [ ] plastic wrap
- [ ] newspaper
- [ ] tongs/rubber gloves

> **WARNING**
> **Wear gloves. Use tongs.**
> **Wash hands.**

(b) *Method:*

- [ ] Half fill the jar with soil.
- [ ] Add four or five different pieces of garbage and make a note of them.
- [ ] Cover the garbage with more soil.
- [ ] Sprinkle the soil with water.
- [ ] Cover the top with plastic wrap.
- [ ] Place the jar in a warm place for a week to ten days.
- [ ] Empty the contents onto newspaper and examine the garbage.

---

2. Record the changes that occurred to each type of garbage on a separate sheet of paper.

3. Answer the questions to make conclusions based on the experiment.

   (a) Which materials began to decompose?

   _____

   (b) Which materials did not decompose very well?

   _____

   (c) From the results of your experiment, which materials should be sent to landfill sites and which could be composted at home?

Landfill Site	*Compost at Home*

> **Fact File**
> *In the 1700s, there were no specific garbage dumping areas. Instead, people threw their garbage into the streets for pigs and other animals to eat!*

Indicators

- *Reads information and answers questions about pesticides.*
- *Identifies and illustrates pesticides used in the family home and suggests safer alternatives.*

Worksheet Information

- Students may need time to understand that finding the balance between the benefits and risks associated with pesticides is not easy, particularly in light of considerable, immediate, economic advantages and lack of indisputable scientific information. This is often further complicated when possible long-term risks are under consideration which may lead some people to choose to ignore or reject them as irrelevant. (Parallels can be made with cigarette smoking.) It is suggested that students are given opportunities to discuss how pesticides affect them now, how they may affect in the future and what they can do about the problem.

- Before completing page 74, students should be encouraged to identify and list the different pesticides found in their homes and to compare their lists with those of others.

- Quiz questions relating to this section may be found on page 16.

Answers

page 76

1. Answers may include:
    (a) sore eyes, sore throats, dizziness, nausea or vomiting, and breathing difficulties
    (b) cancers, immune system damage and birth defects
    (c) The long-term effects have yet to be seen and there is insufficient conclusive research.
2. (a) to destroy or discourage insects, weeds, fungi and diseases
    (b) chemical being spread outside the intended area, often by wind
    (c) Air, soil, or water pollution can result.

3. Ground water pollution can kill animals and plants and make water unfit to drink.
4. Teacher check

page 75

1. Teacher check
2. Teacher check
3. Teacher check

Cross-Curricular Activities

- Debate: "Children are the most vulnerable to pesticides, but they are unable to do anything about it."
- Research organic food, then write an exposition in favor of or against it.

What Are Pesticides?

Pesticides are poisons designed to prevent, destroy, repel or reduce pests, including insects, plants, fungi and diseases.

What Are the Problems?

There are two major problems with pesticides. The first is the ever-increasing use of a multitude of different pesticides, and the second, that we are unsure of their effects on our environment and health, particularly in the long term.

Finding the Balance

It is not easy to balance the benefits and risks of using pesticides. The economic value of agricultural chemicals is significant. They are used to improve the quality and quantity of food and increase overseas exports.

Pesticide is often sprayed to reduce the numbers of particular insects, for example, mosquitoes, and to prevent the spread of potentially fatal diseases, like malaria and encephalitis.

Many homes are regularly sprayed to kill termites or deadly spiders and we may use pesticide sprays to reduce the number of over-friendly flies wishing to share our food and spread disease and infection! Keen gardeners may eradicate weeds and keep their plants and lawns looking beautiful with the aid of pesticides. Pesticides are extremely useful, but at what cost to our environment?

Pesticides and the Environment

One problem that occurs with pesticides is spray drift, usually in rural areas, where wind or other factors result in chemicals being sprayed outside the intended area. Air, water, or ground pollution can occur, often because farmers have not considered the strength or direction of the wind.

Dangerous pesticides are sometimes used when safer alternatives are available because of people's lack knowledge and understanding of the risks.

Some pesticides can remain in the air, soil, or water for a long time and affect other organisms.

Using too much of a pesticide or using it too often, especially before it rains, can cause problems. Excess garden pesticide can be washed into street drains and into waterways where it can create harmful combinations which kill fish and frogs and cause plant-destroying algae. Pesticides in the soil can affect small creatures like earthworms and can enter the groundwater, making it unfit to drink.

Health Issues

Anything that affects the environment has the potential to be a health hazard. Some of the short-term effects of pesticides include sore eyes and throats, dizziness, nausea, and breathing difficulties. Long-term effects are of more concern because they harder to detect, so some people are unaware of the dangers or don't want to know about them. These can include cancer, damage to the immune system and birth defects. Children are particularly vulnerable to the effects of pesticides.

Overcoming the Problem

Many people believe that education and information based on scientific research are the keys to combating the problems caused by pesticides. If people understand the problems and dangers, they will be more likely to protect the environment and their families' health.

Pesticides - 2

Answer the questions using the text provided on page 73.

1. (a) What are some of the short-term effects of pesticides on people's health?

_____

(b) What are some of the possible long-term effects?

_____

(c) Why do you think people don't know about the long-term effects of some pesticides?

_____

_____

2. (a) Why do farmers use pesticides?

_____

(b) What is spray drift?

_____

(c) Why can spray drift be dangerous?

_____

_____

3. Explain why pesticide in groundwater can be harmful.

_____

_____

4. Complete the chart, listing some of the benefits and risks of pesticides.

Benefits of Pesticides	*Risks of Pesticides*

Fact File

It has been claimed that an average apple could have as many as four pesticides on it, even after it has been washed.

1. Think about all the pesticides used in your house or garden to kill or discourage insects or unwanted plants. Complete the table.

PEST	LOCATION	PESTICIDE	Frequency of Use			
			daily	weekly	monthly	annually

2. (a) Which pesticide do you think is the most dangerous?

_____

(b) Why? _____

_____

_____

_____

3. (a) Which pesticide do you think could be replaced with something less dangerous?

_____

(b) Explain how the alternative works and why it is less dangerous.

_____

_____

_____

_____

> **Fact File**
>
> *Predictions have been made that estimate a 30 percent increase in cancer over the next ten years. Pesticides are considered to be one of the risk factors.*

Indicators

- *Reads information and answers questions about hazardous waste.*
- *Researches to write, follow and evaluate a procedure to produce a nontoxic household cleaner.*

Worksheet Information

- Students will benefit from opportunities to examine the types of hazardous waste produced by different businesses and industries, their current disposal methods and those used in the past. The track records of many companies have been very poor and students need some understanding of the economic and technological reasons for this. They also need to understand that many people did not really understand, believe or care about the magnitude or seriousness of the long-term problems they were causing to health and the environment.

- Before students are required to complete the exercise on page 79, they may need to review the type of information provided in a procedure and how it is organized and presented.

- Quiz questions relating to this section may be found on page 17.

Answers

page 78

1. (a) air, soil and water

   (b) Hazardous waste is unwanted material with the potential to cause harm to the environment or humans.

2. (a) Flammable products are those which ignite easily.

   (b) Toxic products are those which, when inhaled, ingested or absorbed, can cause death or injury.

3. (a) and (b) Teacher check

4. Answers may include:

   (a) Buying only the quantity needed, Giving excess to others.

   (b) Increase awareness by reading labels carefully and being more selective.

   (c) Store upright in original container, away from children and separated from other hazardous material.

   (d) Research, time and effort

5. (a) and (b) Teacher check

page 79

Teacher check

Cross-Curricular Activities

- Choose a particular hazardous waste and design and create a poster to show how it can be reduced or managed.

- Research how and why plastic bags are harmful to sea creatures and write a report.

- Working in small groups, use the words "hazardous waste" to write an acrostic which shows an understanding of the concept.

What Is Hazardous Waste?

Hazardous waste is unwanted material that has the potential to cause either short-term or long-term harm to the environment or people. It is linked to industrialization, and it is, unfortunately, often a by-product of necessary development.

Hazardous waste can seep into groundwater, contaminate soil and escape into the air. It can cause problems in ocean environments, where aquatic animals, including dolphins, have been adversely affected by waste from the fishing and other industries.

Characteristics of Hazardous Waste

Hazardous material can be one or more of the following:

- **Toxic** – Death or injury can be caused by inhalation, ingestion or absorption.
- **Corrosive** – Living tissue or other materials can be eaten away, burned, or destroyed.
- **Flammable** – Products can ignite easily and lead to fires.
- **Reactive** – Explosion may result from pressure, heat or shock.
- **Infectious** – Bacterial infections can be transmitted by medical waste.
- **Radioactive** – The disposal of radioactive medical waste is a concern for some hospitals.

Managing Hazardous Waste

The dangers of hazardous waste are not well understood by the community. Even scientific opinions vary, making it difficult to reach agreement and to put effective management policies into place. Cost is also a critical factor for business, industrial and community management.

Three key management strategies are:

1. Reduce the amount of hazardous waste.
2. Choose less hazardous products.
3. Improve environmentally responsible storage and waste disposal.

Hazardous Household Waste (HHW)

Although hazardous wastes result from business and industry, there are many to be found in our homes, garages and sheds. Some of the most common HHW's include: cleaning and polishing chemicals, gasoline and kerosene, pool chemicals, batteries, pesticides, paint, nail polish and polish removers, oven and drain cleaners, and mothballs.

We should try to apply the three key management strategies in our own homes, because we *can* make a difference to the environment and to our health.

Strategy 1

We shouldn't buy more of a product than we require, and if there is an excess, we could offer it to someone who will use it.

Strategy 2

If we read the labels carefully to identify nontoxic or biodegradable products, we should be able to be more selective about the products we choose. There are also a number of nontoxic products that can be substituted for many cleaners; for example, baking soda, white vinegar, lemon juice and salt.

Strategy 3

It is important to store hazardous waste in its original container and to make sure that the container is upright and tightly closed. Ensure that it is in a safe place, away from heat, separated from flammable or corrosive products and beyond the reach of small children. Responsible HHW disposal may require some research to find out what to do, perhaps from your local council, and some time and effort to follow their instructions. It is really important to do this so we can save our environment and protect our health.

Answer the questions using the text on page 77.

1. (a) Which three aspects of the environment can be affected by hazardous waste?

(b) What is hazardous waste? _____

_____

_____

2. Explain what is meant by:

(a) Flammable _____

(b) Toxic _____

3. (a) Name three hazardous products that are kept at your home.

(b) Choose one and describe how it should be stored and disposed of safely.

_____

_____

4. How can we:

(a) Reduce hazardous household waste?

_____

_____

(b) Choose less hazardous products?

_____

_____

(c) Improve storage of hazardous household waste?

_____

_____

(d) Improve the disposal of hazardous household waste?

_____

_____

5. (a) Which hazardous waste causes you the most concern?

_____

(b) Why? _____

_____

_____

Fact File

Americans throw away billions of plastic bags a year. A plastic bag can take up to 1,000 years to break down.

Nontoxic Solutions

Research to find a recipe for an alternative nontoxic general household cleaner. Use the plan below to write a procedure for making this product. Make the product and use it as directed. Test your product. Does it work?

Title:

Goal:

Materials:

Method:

Test results:

Fact File

Asbestos products are no longer used as they are an extreme health hazard. There is no way of treating or recycling asbestos waste, and the only way to immobilize and dispose of it is to bury it as landfill.

Water Resources

Indicators

- *Reads information on and answers questions about water resources.*
- *Calculates, averages, compares and graphs water consumption data.*

Worksheet Information

- Discuss the location and purpose of, and how, when and by whom students' water meters are read. Find out if there is a meter located at the school.

- Students will need to analyze and become familiar with the information provided in the different sections of the water account on page 83 and would benefit from opportunities to compare it with other water accounts. Some students may be able to complete the calculations required in this activity independently, but others may benefit from working in small groups to solve the math problem.

- Graph paper is required for this activity.

- Quiz questions relating to this section may be found on page 17.

Answers

Page 82

1. (a) solid or ice, liquid or water, gas or water vapor

   (b) Almost the same amount of water is recycled by evaporation and precipitation.

   (c) Most evaporation occurs over the oceans.

   (d) 97 percent

   (e) It is frozen in the polar ice caps and in glaciers.

2. Teacher check

3. (a) Most of the water used in agriculture is for irrigation.

   (b) covering channels to reduce evaporation, irrigating at night, cultivating crops needing less water, charging more for the water

4. Teacher check

Page 83

1. 3,458 gal

2. 447.8 gal

   Possible calculation:

   2,952 + 2,883 + 3,233 + 3,175 + 3,247 + 3,313 + 3,184 + 3,089 = 25,076 gal

   (This is the amount of water used in 8 weeks.)

   25,076 divided by 8 = 3,134.5 gal is the amount used in 1 week.

   3,134.5 divided by 7 = 447.8 gal is the amount used in 1 day.

3. (a) Yes, they saved 494 – 447.8 = 46.2 gal per day.

   (b) Teacher check – see above.

4. Teacher check. (Weeks should be shown on the X axis and consumption on the Y axis.)

Cross-Curricular Activities

- Compile a list of rules to help a family conserve water in their house and garden.

- Design a poster promoting water quality.

- Research salinity and write a report about what causes it. Suggest some possible ways of dealing with it.

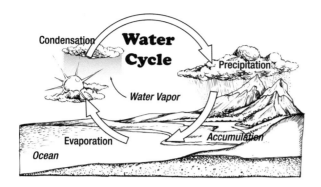

The Earth's Water

All life on our planet depends on water. Water is the only substance on Earth that occurs in the three different forms or states: solid (ice), liquid (water) and gas (water vapor).

Water is an almost constant, limited resource, in what can be described as a "closed system." This means that most of the same water is recycled through the atmosphere about every eight days as precipitation (rain or snow) and then evaporates into the atmosphere again, mainly from the oceans.

Only a very small amount of the Earth's water is available for humans to use, because over 97 percent is the salt water of the world's oceans and although a further 2 percent is fresh water, it is frozen in the polar ice caps and glaciers. This leaves less than 1 percent, which is found in lakes, rivers and groundwater, for the Earth's growing population to use.

Water Quality

Water is an excellent solvent, which makes it very vulnerable to pollution from many sources, including:

- *Organic matter* from livestock manure and human sewage, which decomposes, lowering oxygen in the water and killing plants and animals.
- *Biological pollutants* like cholera and typhoid, which increase when organic matter is present.
- *Pesticides and fertilizers* from agriculture and domestic sources, which enter lakes, rivers, oceans and underground water, particularly where there is insufficient topsoil to filter them.

- *Heavy metals*, like mercury, lead and cadmium, resulting from industrial processes, which can settle on the bottom of streams. In Minamata, Japan, during the 1950s, an accumulation of methyl mercury in fish and shellfish from industry affected over 3,000 victims.
- *Oil spills* from tankers which have damaged and destroyed coastal environments and aquatic animals and birds.
- *Thermal pollution* from water which has been used to cool machinery and is then discharged into waterways, heating the water and reducing its ability to hold the oxygen needed to support flora and fauna.

Many of the world's population do not have access to unpolluted drinking water, either from surface or underground sources. This problem is increasing at an alarming rate as underground contamination can spread over considerable distances. Water often has chemicals like chlorine added, or it is filtered or boiled to avoid disease.

Water pollution also puts the world's ecosystems under stress, because water is essential for all life.

Water Conservation

Most water is needed by agriculture to produce food. Irrigation uses 70 percent of this water, some of which could be saved by covering channels to reduce evaporation, irrigating at night, or growing crops needing less water.

Industry is the second largest consumer. Savings could be made by recycling water and changing some of the materials used.

Domestic water use continues to increase, and there are many ways it can be reduced, including replacing water-hungry lawns and gardens, using more water-efficient appliances, toilets and showers, improved detection of leaks and educating people about water conservation.

One of the more effective ways of reducing water consumption has been found to be increasing the cost of water to consumers, including farmers. This makes them more efficient users of this precious resource.

Answer the questions using the text on page 81.

1. (a) Name the three different forms in which water occurs.

   _____

   (b) The Earth's water can be described as a *closed system*. Explain what this means.

   _____

   _____

   (c) Where does most of the Earth's evaporation take place?

   _____

   _____

   (d) What percentage of the Earth's water is salty?_____

   (e) Why is 2 percent of the Earth's fresh water not available for drinking or agriculture?

   _____

2. Name two sources of water pollution and describe how each affects water quality.

Pollutant:	Pollutant:
Effect on water quality:	**Effect on water quality:**

3. (a) How is most of the water needed for agriculture used?_____

   (b) How could some of this water be saved?

   _____

   _____

4. Describe three ways to reduce the amount of water used for domestic pupuses.

   • _____

   • _____

   • _____

┌─ **Fact File** ─────────────────────────────────

Restoration of contaminated underground water can take tens, hundreds, or in some cases, even tens of thousands of years. It is a problem we cannot afford to

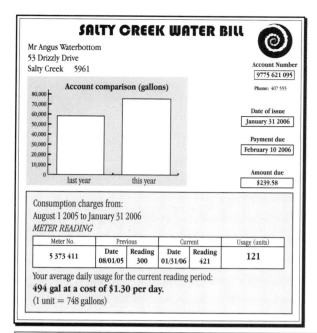

SALTY CREEK WATER BILL

Mr Angus Waterbottom
53 Drizzly Drive
Salty Creek 5961

Account comparison (gallons)

Account Number
9775 621 095

Phone: 407 555

Date of issue
January 31 2006

Payment due
February 10 2006

Amount due
$239.58

Consumption charges from:
August 1 2005 to January 31 2006
METER READING

Meter No.	Previous		Current		Usage (units)
	Date	Reading	Date	Reading	
5 373 411	08/01/05	300	01/31/06	421	121

Your average daily usage for the current reading period:
494 gal at a cost of $1.30 per day.
(1 unit = 748 gallons)

Do you know how much water your family uses a day and how much it costs?

Talon had never really thought about it until his dad said he would have to wait until next month to get the new skateboard he'd promised him. Dad explained that he was really sorry, but he had the water bill to pay and just didn't have the money. Talon checked out the bill on the fridge and was amazed to discover that it was for $239.58 and they really *did* have to pay for the water they used. He'd learned about water conservation and knew how important it was, so he decided to make a plan to reduce his family's water use and their bill.

Talon's Plan

- Set a goal of saving 30 gallons each day.
- Write a list of ways the family can conserve water in their house and garden, tell them about it, then display the list on the fridge.
- Read the water meter each week and record the number of gallons used.

Weekly Water Use (in gallons)			
Week 1	Week 2	Week 3	Week 4
2952	2883	3233	3175
Week 5	Week 6	Week 7	Week 8
3247	3313	3184	3089

1. Use the information provided on the water account to work out the family's average weekly water consumption in gallons.

   _____

2. Use Talon's recorded weekly consumption to calculate their average daily consumption, in gallons, over the eight weeks. (You may use the back of this sheet for your calculations.)

   _____

3. Did Talon's family achieve their goal of saving an average of 30 gallons each day?

   _____

4. On a sheet of graph paper, use Talon's recordings to graph the family's weekly water consumption over the eight-week period.

Show all your calculations. Use another sheet if required.

Fact File

The diversion of streams flowing into the Aral Sea for irrigation resulted in the reduction of flora and fauna, local climate change, increased wind erosion, the extinction of some species and the loss of a major fishing industry. This is because the volume of water in the sea has been reduced by two-thirds and salinity has increased. It is estimated that the Aral Sea could be gone by the year 2020.

Tsunamis — Ring of Fire

Indicators

- *Reads information and answers questions about the Ring of Fire.*
- *Learns why the majority of submarine earthquakes and tsunamis occur in the Ring of Fire.*

Worksheet Information

- Seismic activity refers to earthquakes. Scientists have developed a theory called plate tectonics which explains the geological features and activities occurring at the Earth's crust. The extreme temperatures and pressures that exist when oceanic plates collide can result in the formation of chains of violent volcanoes, such as the Ring of Fire.
- There are six major volcanic areas in the Ring of Fire.
- A tsunami may also occur in a fjord, a narrow inlet surrounded by cliffs. A fjord tsunami may be generated when a portion of iceberg breaks, or calves, into the water. The resulting wave pattern is different from that created by a submarine earthquake in an ocean tsunami.
- Quiz questions relating to this section may be found on page 18.

Answers

page 34

1. Teacher check
2. earthquakes
3. (a) false (b) true (c) false (d) true (e) true
4. Teacher check
5. (a)

E	N	E	R	G	Y	T	H	E	R	C	N
A	I	N	G	L	T	O	F	A	I	O	F
R	O	A	Y	O	I	M	K	N	N	R	E
T	G	E	B	I	S	A	E	S	L	A	
H	S	N	A	A	C	M	N	I	N	L	
Q	E	I	G	L	L	O	A	H	U	T	E
U	I	X	A	O	N	U	C	R	P	S	U
A	S	O	V	E	F	A	L	E	L	P	T
K	M	B	H	C	I	F	I	C	A	P	I
E	I	P	H	E	N	O	M	T	N	A	
A	C	T	I	V	I	T	Y	R	E	E	N
N	S	U	B	M	A	R	I	N	E	O	N

(b) the Ring of Fire is a natural phenomenon.

Cross-Curricular Activities

- Students draw up a time line of major recorded tsunamis, including a legend to illustrate the ocean in which each occurred.
- Students collect data from major recorded tsunamis to determine the top five. They may choose their own criteria for determining this; e.g., loss of life, strength of earthquake, greatest distance between earthquake and tsunami.
- Students research the tectonic plates in the Pacific region and label them on a map. They research how movement of and collisions between these plates have caused some well-known geographical features.

page 35

Teacher check

Ring of Fire - 1 — Tsunamis

The **Ring of Fire** is an arc marking an area of great volcanic and seismic activity. It is located around the edges of the Pacific Ocean, extending north from New Zealand, along the eastern edge of Asia, east towards the Aleutian Islands off the coast of Alaska and south along the entire length of both American continents.

The Earth's crust is covered with a number of irregularly-shaped plates which can move and collide with each other, generating massive amounts of energy. This energy can result in the formation of volcanoes and the occurrence of submarine earthquakes. If an earthquake is powerful enough, a tsunami may be generated.

The Ring of Fire lies where the Pacific Plate is colliding with other plates. Although tsunamis are a global phenomenon, they occur most frequently in the Pacific Ocean.

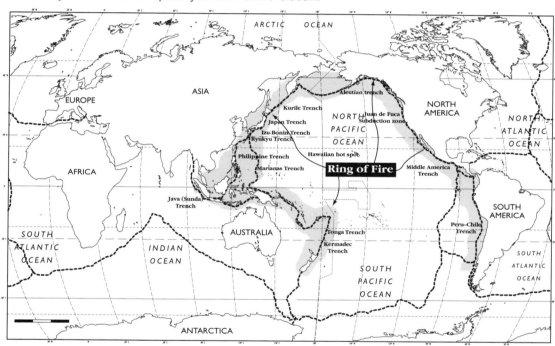

This list shows some of the major Ring of Fire tsunamis caused by earthquakes.

1946 – The Aleutian Island earthquake generated a tsunami which badly affected the coast of Alaska and also the Hawaiian islands in the mid-Pacific. Following this disaster, a tsunami warning system was established for countries in the area of the Pacific Ocean.

1960 – The Great Chilean earthquake, reaching 9.5 on the Richter scale, caused one of the most devastating tsunamis of the 20th century. Almost 24 hours after the earthquake, the tsunami hit the coast of Japan on the other side of the ocean.

1964 – The Good Friday earthquake in Alaska caused tsunamis which hit areas along the whole length of the North American coast.

The most destructive tsunami on record occurred on Boxing Day, 2004, in the Indian Ocean. From Indonesia, Thailand and Malaysia, close to the earthquake, to Bangladesh, India, Sri Lanka and the Maldives, thousands of miles away, over 300,000 people died. Kenya, Somalia and Tanzania, on the east coast of Africa, were also affected. This was the first major tsunami in the Indian Ocean since the eruption of Krakatoa in 1883.

Tsunamis **Ring of Fire - 2**

Answer the questions using the text on page 33.

1. Why do you think the Ring of Fire was given its name? _____

    _____

2. What natural phenomenon do you think a seismologist studies?

3. Check **true** or **false**.

    (a) The Ring of Fire is located on the edges of the Indian Ocean.   True ◯ False ◯

    (b) The Earth's crust is covered with irregular plates.   True ◯ False ◯

    (c) All submarine earthquakes cause tsunamis.   True ◯ False ◯

    (d) Tsunamis can occur anywhere in the world.   True ◯ False ◯

    (e) A Richter scale measures the strength of an earthquake.   True ◯ False ◯

4. Why do you think a tsunami warning system was established for countries next to the Pacific Ocean but not for those countries adjacent to the Indian Ocean?

    _____

    _____

5. (a) Find these words in the word search. The words may be found in any direction.

Ring of Fire	tsunami	ocean
volcanic	seismic	Aleutian
earthquake	activity	Chile
plate	submarine	Alaska
Pacific	phenomenon	Boxing
energy	global	Day

E	N	E	R	G	Y	T	H	E	R	C	N
A	I	N	G	L	I	O	F	A	I	O	F
R	D	A	Y	O	I	M	K	N	N	R	E
T	I	G	E	B	I	S	A	E	S	L	A
H	S	N	A	A	A	C	M	N	I	N	L
Q	E	I	G	L	L	O	A	H	U	T	E
U	I	X	A	O	N	U	C	R	P	S	U
A	S	O	V	E	F	A	L	E	L	P	T
K	M	B	H	C	I	F	I	C	A	P	I
E	I	P	H	E	N	O	I	M	T	N	A
A	C	T	I	V	I	T	Y	R	E	E	N
N	S	U	B	M	A	R	I	N	E	O	N

    (b) Reading left to right and top to bottom, write the sentence formed from the unused letters.

Fact File

In 1993, seismologists discovered the largest known concentration of volcanoes on the sea floor in the South Pacific – 1,133 volcanoes in an area about half the size of Tasmania!

 86   **ENVIRONMENTAL ISSUES**   ©World Teachers Press®   www.worldteacherspress.com

Ring of Fire Mapping [Tsunamis]

When we hear of natural disasters around the world, it is helpful to know the exact location of the events and the areas affected by them.

1. Using library resources or the Internet, research any three tsunamis within the Ring of Fire. Record each event.

Tsunami Name	Location	Year

2. Label the map with the names of countries, towns and cities affected by the earthquakes and tsunamis.

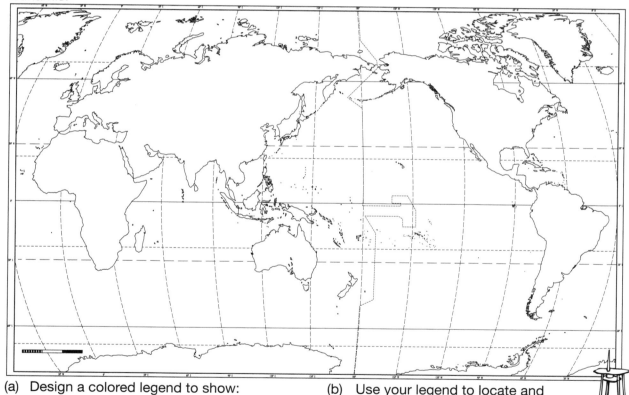

3. (a) Design a colored legend to show:

   Earthquake

   Tsunami

   Direction of tsunami

   (b) Use your legend to locate and illustrate the earthquakes and tsunamis on the map.

Fact File

In 1949, the Pacific Tsunami Warning System was established. From a base in Hawaii, modern technology devices help detect earthquakes that may cause a tsunami.